Teaching the Heathens

The story of schooling in the village of Mannings Heath in the Sussex Parish of Nuthurst in the 19th and 20th Centuries

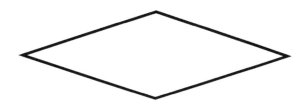

Howard Malleson

All rights reserved
Copyright © Howard Malleson, 2022

The right of Howard Malleson to be identified as the author of this
work has been asserted in accordance with Section 78
of the Copyright, Designs and Patents Act 1988

The book cover is copyright to Howard Malleson

This book is published by
Grosvenor House Publishing Ltd
Link House
140 The Broadway, Tolworth, Surrey, KT6 7HT.
www.grosvenorhousepublishing.co.uk

This book is sold subject to the conditions that it shall not, by way of
trade or otherwise, be lent, resold, hired out or otherwise circulated
without the author's or publisher's prior consent in any form of binding or
cover other than that in which it is published and
without a similar condition including this condition being imposed
on the subsequent purchaser.

A CIP record for this book
is available from the British Library

ISBN 978-1-83975-891-1

Contents

Chapters

	Prologue	vii
1	An Introduction to the Story	1
2	Time Line – *what happened and when*	2
3	Early Days – *times of growing political concern*	4
4	Setting the Scene – *Mannings Heath in the early 1800s*	7
5	The Swing Riots – *revolt of agricultural labour in the 1830s*	15
6	Then Came the Methodists – *arrival in Mannings Heath and the first chapel and school*	31
7	1832, the First School – *the beginnings of "Teaching the Heathens"*	37
8	A Ferment of Activity – *towards compulsory universal education*	43
9	1869, the Second Chapel – *and the beginnings of the Wesleyan/Methodist Elementary School*	46
10	1870, the Wesleyan/Methodist Elementary School – *and the emergence of William Reading*	55
11	The Small, Private School	67
12	The Forest School, Coolhurst	69
13	1883, The Birth of the Church of England School in Mannings Heath	73
14	1883/4, the First Academic Year	82
15	Reflections of the First Year of the Mannings Heath School	92
16	1884/5, the Second Academic Year – *and what a difference*	99
17	September 1885/April 1887, the Third Academic Year – *and the arrival and departure of Louisa Buck*	104
18	May 1887/May 1913, the Return of Louisa – *and real progress*	108
19	May 1913/April 1922, A Time of War – *signs of major change*	125
20	April 1922/November 1924 – *the battle for Mannings Heath School*	134

21	December 1923/January 1926 – *the aftermath of the battle*	148
22	January 1926/January 1939 – *a period of stability in the life of Mannings Heath School*	153
23	1939/1945 – *the war years*	173
24	The End – *1946 and after*	195
	Epilogue	197

Appendices

1	The Chart Family Genealogy – 1770s to 1940s	201
2	Record of Pupils Joining the Mannings Heath CE/Board School in the First Academic Years 1883/4 and 1884/5	203
3	Mannings Heath CE/Board School – The Head Teachers	209
4	Mannings Heath School Pupils Who Saw Military Service in World War 1	215
5	Pupil Numbers on the School Register	219
6	Reference Sources for Information on Some Major World War 2 Incidents in and Around Mannings Heath	221

References

Acknowledgements

As the author, I have received help and advice from many people – too many to list them all individually.

But, in particular, I would like to thank Tony Turner and Alan Lindfield of the Nuthurst Local History Society for their many and major contributions, and for contributions that have been made by many other Society members. I am grateful to Mark Scrase Dickins for information on Coolhurst and the family's relationship with Mannings Heath and to Jon Quigly for his IT 'life saving' contributions towards reaching the publication stage.

It would not have been possible to write this story without access to many information sources and their staff. I thank the staff of the National Archives at Kew, the East Sussex Record Office at The Fortress, Falmer, the Surrey Record Office, Woking and, in particular, the West Sussex Record Office in Chichester, and the staff of Horsham Museum, especially the Curator, Jeremy Knight.

And last, but by no means least, to my wife, Ann, and my family, who have put up with my immersion in this project over a number of years.

Prologue

The project to research and write the story of "Teaching the Heathens" was identified in 2008 by the Nuthurst Local History Society in West Sussex. As a member of that society, I forgot the dictum "never volunteer" and said that I would take it on.

On the face of it, it looked like a very straightforward task. The school where the Heathens – children from the village of Manning Heath – were taught, opened in 1883 and was closed in 1946, and the complete Head Teacher's log books[1] and the pupil Admissions Register were available. So, what could have been easier as a project?

It was my first venture into the world of local history research so, like the innocent abroad, I got started. It did not take long to find out that "easier as a project" was a complete misnomer and I found myself launched on a real voyage of discovery.

The first discovery was that the Head Teacher's log books told very little of the story – unless one is fascinated by endless mentions of visits from the "nit" nurse and the records of the Attendance Officer and school inspectors. So, nowhere near the useful reference source that I, in my naivety, anticipated. The second discovery that emerged very early on was that "teaching the Heathens" actually began well over fifty years before 1883. This led me to start delving into many other documents and sources, and not just the formal school record.

As a real beginner at historical research, I never anticipated the fascinating side issues that such research would "throw up" and, in my fascination, I could not resist being drawn down many avenues that contained little direct references to the teaching of the Heathens, but also told much about rural village life. I have included many of these stories within this book and I justify so doing on the grounds that it provides you, the reader, with valuable insights into the social and political environment in which the teaching of the Heathens, the children of the village, took place.

Howard Malleson
August, 2021

---

1 Mannings Heath C of E School Head Teacher Log Books 1883-1946.

Chapter 1

An Introduction to the Story

This story does not begin in 1883, but much earlier, and, in fact "teaching the Heathens" begins at least as early as 1832, and possibly even earlier than that. The story of schooling in Mannings Heath does not end in 1946 but continues with the Methodists still teaching the Heathens at Sunday School well into the 1980s.

So the story of schooling in Mannings Heath spans 150 years in the life of a rural Sussex village; through periods of dramatic social change, real development in the way children are educated, wars, including two World Wars, extreme poverty, social unrest, battles between the village and government authorities, parish politics, the major influence of Wesleyanism and Methodism on the life of the village, examples of both differences and collaboration between the churches, acts of real generosity and endeavour by individuals, a long distance love affair and a host of smaller incidents, good and bad; the stuff of real life.

What is contained in the formal and informal records gives us a wonderful and priceless picture of life in a Sussex village through two tumultuous centuries.

Chapter 2

Time Line – *what happened and when*

I have gone back to the early 1800s because, as we will discover, the political and social circumstances when our story begins play major parts in what follows. The time line hints at the great influence that the Wesleyans and Methodists have had on the life of Mannings Heath, and on "teaching the Heathens" … but more of that later.

1819	Publication by the House of Commons of the digest of returns made to the Select Committee appointed to investigate the state of The Education of the Poor. The report is over 3,000 pages of detailed information provided by every parish in England, and the original is housed in the Bodleian Library of Oxford University. (See references 2 and 3.)
1830	Riots by agricultural labourers across the South of England as a result of a lack of work, restrictions on self-sufficiency and increasingly grinding poverty – known as the Swing Riots.
1832	First Wesleyan Chapel opened, on the south side of Golding Lane, in Mannings Heath, which was used as a school and a place of worship.
1841	First comprehensive National Census.
1861	Newcastle Report recommending the provision of "sound and cheap" elementary education; the precursor to the 1870 Education Act.
1869	Second Wesleyan Chapel opened on the north side of Golding Lane, adjacent to the Recreation Ground (now known as the Common).
1870	"Reading's" school opened in the first Wesleyan Chapel. Elementary Education Act (aka the Forester Act) introduced universal education for 5–13-year-olds. It was followed by a number of further Acts in 1873 and 1876, making amendments to the 1870 Act and, in 1879, an Act extending the 1870 act to cover "Industrial Schools". In 1880, the Mundella Act tightened up school attendance laws which had been left a little open in the 1870 Act.

Chapter 2: Time Line – *what happened and when*

1883	Church of England (C of E) school opened in a new building located opposite the Recreation Ground on the south side of Golding Lane.
1884	Pupils from "Reading's" school transferred to the new C of E school. The first Wesleyan Chapel continued to be used as a Methodist Sunday School.
1904	The First Chapel demolished. (Note that the date is an estimate of when demolition took place.)
1946	C of E School closed. Pupils transferred to St Andrew's School in Nuthurst and to other local schools in Horsham and Lower Beeding.
1951	The Methodist National Children's Home (NCH) opened at Forest House in Winterpit Lane. The C of E School building was demolished and two bungalows built on the cleared site. (Note that the date is an estimate of when demolition took place.)
1962	The second Wesleyan Chapel was closed as a place of worship and the Sunday School ceased.
1968	The second Wesleyan Chapel was re-opened and the Sunday School was re-started.
1973	The second Wesleyan Chapel was finally closed as a place of worship and sold for conversion into a dwelling. The Sunday School continued to be provided by Methodist chapel members from Horsham and took place in the National Children's Home and in the Mannings Heath Community Centre (Village Hall).

Chapter 3

Early Days – *times of growing political concern*

The late 1700s and early 1800s saw increasing political concern, discussion, debates and attempts at legislation around the matter of the education of the poor and the underprivileged. In the early 1800s a Select Committee of twenty-seven MPs, under the leadership of Henry Brougham, 1st Baron Brougham and Vaux, carried out a detailed review, across every parish in the land, of the provisions being made for the education of the poor.

Henry Brougham was a Whig politician and reformer, and started his professional life as a Scottish lawyer and founder of the Edinburgh Review.

Henry Brougham MP 1778-1868.

Held office as Lord Chancellor, under Earl Grey, from 1830 to 1834.

Fought against the slave trade and supported free trade with Europe. Proposer and supporter of educational reform and founder of University College London.

As a flavour of his reformist views, and his concerns for the state of the poor, he made a speech in the House of Commons, on what he described as the "state of the nation", on 13th March 1817. The focus of his speech was his concern about the state of the poor, and this is a short extract from the opening:

"Mistaking the symptoms for the malady, we have attempted to stifle the cries of the people in their extreme distress, instead of seeking the cause of their sufferings and endeavouring to apply a cure."

The enactment of the "Gagging Acts" by Parliament in 1817 was a prime example of "stifling the cries" following public unrest by gagging the publication of radical newspapers and satirical magazines, such as The Black Dwarf, rather than addressing the underlying issues that gave them birth.

Chapter 3: Early Days – *times of growing political concern*

In 1818, the Select Committee published the Parochial Returns from every parish in the land[2]. This is a remarkable piece of work in two volumes and amounting to some 3,000 pages. The original is held by the Bodleian Library, Oxford. It contains a vast amount of data, drawn from some 12,000 parishes, that was obtained and collated before the communication and analysis capabilities that we take for granted today.

Amongst the returns was one for the Parish of Nuthurst: -

Population in 1811	539
Poor in 1815	65
Particulars relating to Endowments for Education of Youth	None
Other Institutions for the purpose of Education	A school for boys supported by subscription; also, one for girls, taught by a mistress, who is supported by the parish.
Observations by the Rector T. Valentine	The poor have not the means of paying for the education of their children and are generally desirous of possessing them; and the minister is of the opinion that the necessity of the agricultural labourer applying for parochial relief, will never be obviated till their wages are increased adequate to the increased prices of the necessities of life.

The "Observations" are of particular interest because they are an opportunity for the MPs to determine the underlying feelings in the parishes. The observations were usually made by the Minister or Curate, probably because they were likely to be one of the more literate members of the parish population.

The observations made by the Nuthurst Rector, Thomas Valentine, were in a similar vein to many others. For example, Grinstead, "Most of the poorer classes are without sufficient means of education"; and Horsted Keynes, "The poorer classes are without sufficient means of education and are desirous of possessing them".

Thomas Valentine MD was Rector of Nuthurst, Senior Prebendary of Chichester Cathedral and was also Vicar of Cocking until his death in 1859. He was clearly

---

[2] Parochial Returns made to the Select Committee inquiring about the education of the poor.

a man of "presence" in the county of Sussex and a person whose views would have been respected. He was succeeded, as Rector of Nuthurst, by Rev. John Ommaney McCarogher, who was instituted initially as Curate.

Valentine's words vividly set the scene for the unrest that was to come a few years later in the agricultural parishes of the south of England.

Unfortunately, there is no evidence to tell us where the two Nuthurst schools were located – in Nuthurst itself or in one or more of the four hamlets and villages making up the parish of Nuthurst. Perhaps one was in Mannings Heath, but we do not know.

However, in 1833, the Select Committee carried out a second survey, published in 1835, entitled "Education Enquiry"[3]. The results for Nuthurst are as follows: -

"Nuthurst Parish (population 723) – Three Daily Schools, one whereof, a National School, (commenced 1824), contains 40 males, and is partly supported by subscription and partly by weekly penny payments from the children; in the other two schools are 6 males and 40 females; 25 of the latter are paid for in like manner as the children in the National School, the rest by their parents. - Three Sunday schools, supported by voluntary contributions; in two of which (commenced 1824), are 40 males and 40 females, who attend the Established Church; the other (commenced 1832), consists of about the same number of children (many of whom are from adjoining parishes), and appertains to Wesleyan Methodists."

So, in the period since 1818, the population of Nuthurst had increased by over 30% to 723 and the number of schools had increased by one to three, with the addition of three Sunday Schools, one of which was a Wesleyan Methodist school.

I believe we can draw the following conclusions from these results: -

- The National School that commenced in 1824 is likely to be the Nuthurst St Andrew's School still extant today.
- We do not know where the other two schools were located but they are likely to be the two schools mentioned in the 1818 report.
- The Wesleyan Methodist Sunday School will be the school in the first Mannings Heath Wesleyan Methodist Chapel (see Chapter 6). This is the first positive reference to a school in Mannings Heath.

---

3 Education Enquiry Abstract of the Answers and Returns 1835.

Chapter 4

Setting the Scene – *Mannings Heath in the early 1800s*

So, what was Mannings Heath like in the early 1800s? The tithe map for 1841 shows a small community of about 45 households, with the majority along the track, that is now Pound Lane, and leading to the Dun Horse junction, with what is now the A281. The total population was 183, and about a third were children under 12 years of age[4].

The hamlet was a very close-knit community, with nearly a quarter of the population coming from just two families – the Charts and the Dinnages. Both those names will figure large in the story as it develops.

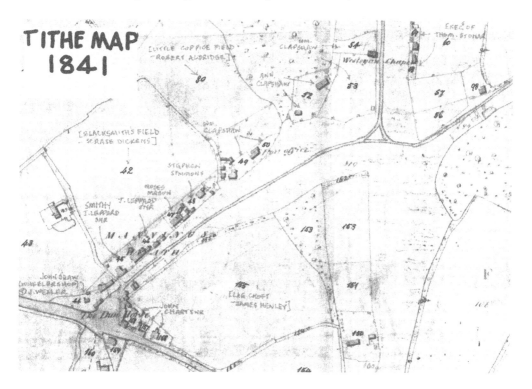

---

[4] 1841 England, Wales and Scotland Census.

Agriculture was the dominant activity within the community, with over 50% of the working males being either agricultural labourers or farmers. There were four blacksmiths, three wheelwrights, three carpenters and two sawyers, all of whom would have been employed, serving the working needs of farming and agriculture. There was a pub, the Dun Horse, a butcher, a baker, a miller, a grocer and broom and shoe makers, all of whom would have been reliant on the agricultural labourers and farmers wages to give them their income in return for the goods and services they provided.

The Old Forge opposite the Dun Horse pub. From a painting by
Henry Browning published in Booklet No. 1 by Nuthurst Local History Society.

Working in a 19th century blacksmith's forge.
This is the forge at Maplehurst in Nuthurst parish.

Chapter 4: Setting the Scene – *Mannings Heath in the early 1800s*

Typical farm labourers in the early 1800s.

The original Dun Horse public house in Mannings Heath at
the junction of Pound Lane and the Brighton Road.

Life for the "Heathens" in the early 1800s was very hard and getting harder; this was a common feature of life in the rural, agricultural counties of South England, in particular, Kent, Sussex, Surrey, Wiltshire, Berkshire and Hampshire. The level of real poverty amongst the rural labouring class was becoming extreme and the support available for the impoverished was grossly overstretched and becoming ineffective.

William Cobbett was a radical, popular journalist who, in 1830, following three years of bad harvests, published his survey of growing poverty in rural southern counties as "Rural Rides"[5]. He wrote "… the farmers feel all the pinching distress, and the still harsher pinchings of anxiety for the future; and the labouring people are suffering in a degree not to be described. God knows how long the peace is to be kept, if this state of things be not put a stop to."

William Cobbett

March 1763 – June 1835

Born in Farnham, Surrey, and in 1832, became MP for Oldham. (That other radical journalist, Winston Churchill, was a candidate to become MP for Oldham.)

In view of what was to come, Cobbett's words were very prescient.

---

5 Rural Rides in the Counties.

Chapter 4: Setting the Scene – *Mannings Heath in the early 1800s*

It was not just three years of bad harvests that caused the grinding poverty of the agricultural labourers, who made up the majority of Mannings Heath wage earners, there were a number of other social, economic and political factors that were at the heart of the troubles. Some of the most significant were: -

- The series of Enclosure Acts between 1770 and 1830 destroyed the ability of agricultural labourers to use common land for grazing a cow and growing vegetables so as to be self-sufficient, with their wages from working for a farmer being to pay for clothes and other household items. Thus, their sense of independence was lost and the labourers were wholly dependent on being employed[6].
- The end of the Napoleonic Wars in 1815 led to the returning soldiers creating a large increase in the available workforce, with there being a resultant loss of work and providing farmers with the opportunity to reduce hourly rates. Poverty relief (the Speenhamland System in which the level of relief was based on the standard of the price of a loaf of bread) was another contributor to reducing rates of pay, because farmers knew that relief through the parish would be available. However, administering officials were often corrupt and, in many cases, the demand for relief was quickly outstripping the ability of the system to provide adequate relief[7].
- The burden of the church financial tithes, replacing earlier goods in kind, payable to the local Church of England parson. Payment was rigorously enforced, whether the worker was a church member or not, and was often far higher than a poor labourer could afford[8].
- The combination of enclosure, surplus labour and increased mechanisation of farming activities, like threshing, meant that agricultural labourers became employed only as casual labour, by the week or for specific tasks like harvesting and hedging. Permanent "living in" employment declined and incomes continued to fall[9].

To illustrate the extent of the growing poverty of agricultural labourers, look at living costs in relation to earnings[10]. Between 1770 and 1830 there had been very little increase in labourer wage rates, which had remained at about 1s 5d per day in Winter and 1s 9d per day in Summer. Usually, the average wage for an agricultural labourer was 8s 4d per week.

---

6 Emptages of Thanet (Five centuries of family history). Published as a website by Susan Morris, 19th May 2013.
7 The Peel Web. Published at www.historyhome.co.uk by Dr Marjie Bloy.
8 Riots and civil disorder in England – 1830 riots.
9 The Peel Web – Rural Unrest in the 1830s. See reference 5 for details.
10 Swing Riots in Sussex. Agrarian Disturbances in the Winter of 1830. Nigel Bowles (BA Thesis), University of Manchester. Held by WSRO as MP1845.

Some basic living costs were: -

	1770	**1830**
Bread	Less than 1d per lb	More than 2d per lb
Meat	3d to 4d per lb	6d to 7d per lb
Butter	4 1/2 d per lb	11d per lb
Cheese	3d per lb	6d per lb
Shoes	8s 6d per pair	12s 6d per pair

In 1830, The Times newspaper estimated that 14s 1d per week was needed for what the newspaper described as "healthy subsistence". The Times went on to say that "At a time when the rich were becoming richer and more numerous, the humble labourer, on the other hand, has experienced a fall in wages and a progressive loss of comforts without example in the records of English privation." Further confirmation of the degree of real poverty comes from the Kent village of Goudhurst[11], where half the population were classed as paupers and were on parish relief, putting further strain on a social support system that could not cope with the extent of real poverty.

Thus, all the ingredients for civil unrest in the southern agricultural counties were present for William Cobbett's concerns to become real events. The populace had also seen that a revolt in France, in July 1830, had succeeded and led to the replacement of Charles X by Louis Phillipe, the "Citizen King". Almost invariably, unrest in France would spark unrest in neighbouring countries, particularly if it had succeeded. And so, the time was ripe for southern England, with all its growing poverty amongst the agricultural labourers, to rise up in revolt.

It was the introduction of the mechanical threshing machines that was the final "trigger". Traditionally, it was in the winter months that agricultural labourers earned their wages from the manual threshing of corn, flailing, for flour making. This provided an income when other employment was not available. The introduction of machinery, replacing manual labour, meant that less labour was required and a desperately needed income source would disappear. This was a clear example of the industrial revolution directly impacting the well-being of agricultural labourers and the rural labouring poor.

---

11 Captain Swing Riots 1830. West Sussex History No. 63, April 1999.

Chapter 4: Setting the Scene – *Mannings Heath in the early 1800s*

Traditional winter threshing – flailing – of corn for flour,
and then bread making, in the early 1800s.

An early mechanical threshing machine, circa 1790. The result was
a large increase in production of corn, for flour making, with fewer labourers.

It would not be long before power was provided by a horse, further increasing production and reducing manpower.

An early powered threshing machine with the power coming from a harnessed horse. The drawing is of a French machine, but they became common place in England in the early 1800s from France, but similar machines were in use in England by 1830.

Steam threshing machine in operation in Berkshire in 1830.

Chapter 5

The Swing Riots – *revolt of agricultural labour in the 1830s*

It was on the night of Saturday 28th August 1830, that the dam finally burst and the first of the hated threshing machines was destroyed in East Kent. This event marked the beginning of the Swing Riots and, by the third week of October, more than one hundred machines had been destroyed in East Kent. The riots spread rapidly through the arable agricultural counties of the South East and, by the end of the year, had reached East Anglia[12].

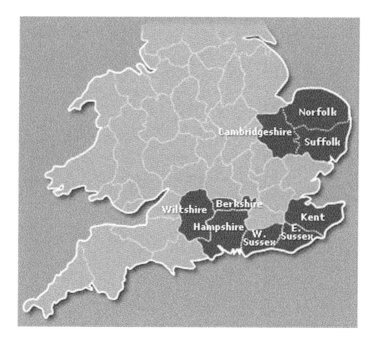

The spread of the Swing Riots through the arable agricultural counties of South and East England in the second half of 1830 (From ref. 10.).

---

12 Swing Riots – the growth of political rights in Britain in the 19th century.

The actions of the rioters took three forms: -

- Physical destruction of threshing and other agricultural machinery.
- Arson attacks on barns and ricks.
- Wages meetings and radical agitation.

Rioting was intense and extensive throughout Sussex[13], and it all happened in a matter of about two months, starting in November 1830. The rioting parishes included Arundel, Felpham, Yapton, Coldwaltham, Wisborough Green, Angmering, East Preston, Petworth, Billingshurst, Pulborough, Bersted, Bosham, East Dean, Singleton... and others. The rioting was extensively reported in the Brighton Gazette[14], for East and West Sussex, in the months of November and December 1830 and January 1831.

Farmers and land owners were sometimes warned of impending attacks by Swing gangs by means of letters sent in the name of "Captain Swing", with the authorities also putting out advertisements in an effort to apprehend the rioters.

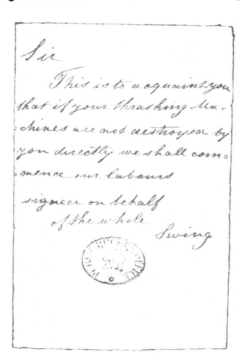

Swing rioter's letter warning the landowner that, if he does
not destroy his threshing machine, the rioters will do it for him.

---

13 The causes of the Swing Riots. Jonathan Nason. BSc dissertation at University of Birmingham, April 1973.
14 Brighton Gazette news cuttings held by the WSRO.

Chapter 5: The Swing Riots – *revolt of agricultural labour in the 1830s*

A poster seeking information on rioters and offering a reward which amounted to about two years earnings for a labourer – a very substantial sum.

The Swing Riots, although originally confined to a limited part of England, attracted widespread attention and figured large in the national press, with the Times, in particular, giving the riots many column inches.

Captain Swing became a name used in many parts of England, to focus attention on hardships and protests. The cartoon[15] overleaf is one example of the wider view of Captain Swing.

---

15 Finding Captain Swing: Protest, Parish Relations and the State of the Public Mind in 1830.

> Canterbury 22d Septr 1830
>
> Sir,
>
> I am directed by the Magistrates of the County of Kent residing near Canterbury to state to you that the destruction of Thrashing Machines has been carried on to a most alarming extent in this part of the County.
>
> These Offences appear to have been committed at midnight by a desperate Gang amounting to upwards of 200 persons.
>
> The Magistrates are using every exertion to discover the Offenders But owing to intimidation they find great difficulty in procuring any Evidence on which they can proceed against the parties.
>
> A General Meeting of County Magistrates acting in East Kent will be held at Canterbury on Saturday next, When they will be happy to receive any communication or advice which you may think proper to offer them.
>
> I have the Honor to be
> Sir
> Your most Humble Servant
>
> Charles Sandys
> Clerk to the Magistrates.

The machinery of the law became involved right from the start and the letter, from the Clerk to East Kent Magistrates, shows that the forces of law and order were beginning to react to the disturbances.

The scale of the riots can be gauged from the numbers of rioters arrested and tried. In total, ref. 7 states that 1,976 rioters were tried with the following results: -

Sentenced to death	252
Commuted to life transportation	233
Executed	19
Transported	505
Imprisoned	644
Fined or whipped	8
Acquitted or bound over	800

For some of those transported, it became their salvation and a route out of the grinding poverty of labourers in southern England. A prime example is William Dove from Norfolk[16].

- He led a Norfolk gang breaking a threshing machine.
- He was caught, tried and sentenced to seven years transportation.
- Transported to Tasmania on the Proteus prison ship along with 250 other criminals.
- In Hobart, he was given a free pardon in 1836 and, in 1838, married Sarah Stanhope; a fellow convict.
- Became the licensee of the "Dog and Partridge" on 1st September 1846 in Barrack Street, Hobart, and started buying and selling properties.
- In 1861, he bought Oakwood for £3,250. Oakwood was a 500-acre estate with the "big house" having 12 bedrooms and a servant's cottage, stabling and a further worker's cottage.
- He died in 1866 as a man of wealth and real substance in the Hobart community.

---

16 Machine Breakers News.

Chapter 5: The Swing Riots – *revolt of agricultural labour in the 1830s* 21

Oakwood – the main house owned by William Dove in 1861.
The house was built in 1842.

Joseph Alexander was another rioter who prospered after transportation[17]. He was part of a Wiltshire group of rioters who destroyed chaff cutting and threshing machines in Ramsbury in November 1830. Other gang members included his brother, Matthias, and his cousin Joseph Liddiard. They were all sentenced to seven years transportation and left for Tasmania on the prison ship Eliza on 2nd February 1831, along with 221 other convicts. They arrived on 29th May of the same year.

Joseph appears to have prospered. He married Ann and had at least one son. The family became hotel owners in Table Cape, with Joseph owning the Court House Hotel and his son, also Joseph, owning the Table Cape Hotel. Joseph died aged 72 in May 1878, and is buried in the family cemetery in Table Cape.

So, in all of this turbulence, what of Mannings Heath – the "Heathens"? There are no records of any Nuthurst parishioners, including our own "Heathens", being participants in the riot incidents; most of the disturbances, centring around Horsham, seem to be meetings and gatherings aimed at winning increases in wages and reducing tithes. There is some evidence that farmers in Nuthurst were sympathetic to the plight of their workers. There is, however, a witness

---

17 British Convict Transportation Registers.

record of arson very close to Horsham. It was witnessed on 16th November 1830, by passengers on the London to Brighton mail coach.

The Heathens must have been well aware of what was happening across the county. In 1830, there were 281 incidents in Sussex alone[18]. The incidents were a mixture of arson (65), assemblages (141), threats of violence, machine breakages and animal mutilation (59), and miscellaneous, local issues (16). The assemblages were usually about increasing wage payments, continuity of employment and reduced tithes. The assemblages were also used by local "politicians" to promote their own agendas.

Some Heathens may well have taken part in the huge gathering in Horsham (ref. 8) reported in the Brighton Guardian newspaper on 25th November 1830, and recorded in the History of the House of Commons for the period 1820-1832[19].

This gathering took place on Friday 18th November, which was the day of the Vestry to appoint the Assistant Overseer who would be responsible for administering the distribution, from the tithes, of financial support to impoverished labourers. The Vestry took place in the Horsham Parish Church, and by 2pm, some 1,500 labourers had assembled at the Church, according to the Brighton Guardian. They demanded the presence of all the big land owners, and when they noticed that Robert Hurst of Horsham Park was not present a group went to fetch him. He was 80 years old at the time, so likely to be fearful of the attentions of a large, angry mob. The other leading land owners present at the Vestry were Henry Tredcroft of Warnham Court and Robert Aldridge of St Leonard's House.

---

18 Popular Protest in South-East England 1790-1840.
19 History of the House of Commons 1820-1832.

Chapter 5: The Swing Riots – *revolt of agricultural labour in the 1830s*

Horsham Park. The home of Robert Hurst MP.

The mob's demand was given, in writing, to the Vestry Clerk, who read it out to the land owners. It read, "We want the rents lowered, the tithes lowered and our wages raised to 2s 6d a day. And your petitioners will every pray."

It seems as though Robert Hurst took it upon himself to lead the land owners response, which was along the lines of needing to think about it and not being able to give an answer that day. This enraged the mob and Henry Tredcot tried to defuse the angry situation by saying that he was sympathetic but could not agree to an increase in wages under the threat and language of intimidation.

By this time, the size of the gathering had increased to a reported 2,000 to 3,000 people, including youngsters, and the level of anger was rising. These numbers need to be treated with some discretion. Jeremy Knight[20] points out that numbers at this gathering ranged from less than 1,000 to about 2,000, depending on when, and to whom, the numbers were being reported. nevertheless, for a quiet market town, the number was substantial; the authorities were concerned enough to bring in troops, while the labourers demands were serious and backed by acts of terror across the Southern agricultural counties.

The land owners made attempts to negotiate 2s a day in Winter and 2s 6d a day in Summer. 2s 6d a day represented about a 50% increase of the going rate and gives a very clear picture of the extant poverty level. After much angry argument,

---

20 Horsham's History Vol. 2.

and several fruitless attempts by Robert Hurst to leave the Church, he agreed to the demands and pledged himself to lower rents and tithes. At this point, his friends were able to drag him to safety out of the Church.

After their victory, the mob split into smaller gangs and went around Horsham demanding money from householders and gathering firewood with the threat of setting light to the Church and the Vicarage. This did not happen, but it must have been a frightening time for the residents of Horsham.

The next day, the mob re-assembled and went to the seat of Admiral Sir James Hawkins-Whiteshed of Holbrook Park, demanding that all his men stop work and join them.

Admiral Sir James Hawkins-Whiteshed.

Served in the Napoleonic Wars joining the Channel Fleet in 1799 with his flag on HMS Temeraire, the subject of the famous "Fighting Temeraire" painting by J.M. Turner. In 1821, he became C-in-C, Portsmouth.

Chapter 5: The Swing Riots – *revolt of agricultural labour in the 1830s*

The Admiral refused to let his men stop work to join the mob, but was obviously a better man-manager and negotiator than the land owners in the Church the day before. The Admiral placated the situation by providing the mob with beer to drink.

Rumours began to spread that a large group of rioting labourers from East Kent, the initiators of the Swing Riots, were on their way to join their Horsham "brothers". This possibility clearly worried the authorities and the High Sheriff of Sussex appealed to the Secretary of State, William Lamb, Viscount Melbourne, who had only been in office for eight days, for a troop of soldiers. The High Sheriff was Thomas Sanctuary, who owned The Nunnery at Rusper.

The Nunnery at Rusper; the home of the High Sheriff of Sussex, Thomas Sanctuary.

Subsequently the Sanctuary's sold the Nunnery estate to the Hursts.

Whilst, on the 20th November, 50 horse guards and 100 troopers marched into Horsham, and quietness was restored.

However, the story does not end there. The success of the Horsham labourers in achieving a betterment of their financial situation became known across the county and led to a gathering in Nuthurst (but this news report remains uncorroborated by any other account so must be treated with caution). If it happened, it will have involved the Heathens, and those further afield. Representatives from the Horsham labourers joined a mob in Surrey and it was reported that the Surrey assembly "acted under the direction of the men of Horsham whose commandments they dare not disobey".

The immediate consequences of the Swing Riots were large scale arrests and punishment, including transportation and execution, described in ref. 7, as summarised in the table on page 20.

There is a good chance that some of those transported to Van Dieman's Land (now Tasmania) from Sussex were known to the Heathens; there were 17 from Sussex transported on the ships Eliza and Proteus[21].

The Heathens will have been particularly aware of the execution of Edmund Bushby in Horsham on New Year's Day 1831[22] [23]. Edmund Bushby had been convicted at Lewes Assizes for torching a farmer's wheat in East Preston; he was condemned to be hung at Horsham Gaol for the crime. On the day, word spread far and wide and the *Morning Chronicle* of 4th January reported that "eight to nine hundred persons" came to watch. It is entirely probable that there were Heathens among the crowd, which was largely made up of agricultural labourers.

The execution was described, in stark and graphic detail, in the Sussex Advertiser of 3rd January 1831, by a reporter who clearly witnessed the event.

Horsham Gaol 1775–1845. Located at "Causey Croft" - near the present-day Iron Bridge.

The site of the public execution of Edmund Bushby in 1831.

---

21 Ships Eliza, Proteus and others.
22 Executed Today blog.
23 Capital Punishment UK.

Chapter 5: The Swing Riots – *revolt of agricultural labour in the 1830s*

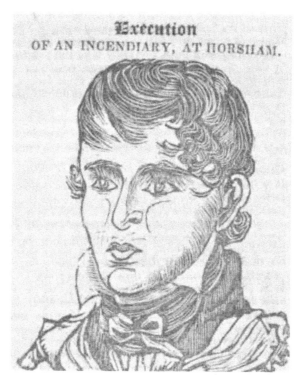

Portrait sketch of Edmund Bushby included in the description
of the execution printed in the Sussex Advertiser of 3rd January 1831.

"EXECUTION OF AN INCENDIARY, AT HORSHAM.

On Saturday last, Edmund Bushby, labourer, aged 26, underwent the extreme penalty of the law, to which he was sentenced at our late assizes, having been found guilty of setting fire to a stack of wheat, the property of George Olliver, at East Preston, in this county.

A respite for fourteen days arrived at Horsham Gaol, on Friday night, for Thomas Goodman, the other unhappy convict, who had been ordered for execution with Busby, for setting fire to the stacks, etc., at Battle. (Authors Note – Goodman escaped execution by confessing and expressing remorse).

At 12 o'clock, Bushby was conducted from the condemned cell, by one of the turn-keys, to the front part of the prison, and thence to the square room on the debtors side of the gaol, where he was delivered over to the executioner. The unhappy criminal conducted himself with the greatest firmness and composure for some minutes, and every preparation being finished with outside, the executioner proceeded to pinion his arms. Bushby, in a firm and impressive manner, exclaimed, "I am now going to another, and I hope to the Lord, a better world!" His neckcloth was then taken off, which the executioner placed in the bosom of the culprit's smock-frock, but he directed for it to be removed, saying - "You had better put that into my hat". This being complied with, Bushby raised his hands, pinioned as he was, towards his mouth, and removed some tobacco and, walking to the opposite side of the room, cast it from him with an air of the greatest composure. All being in readiness, the large folding doors leading to the front of the prison were thrown open, and the solemn procession moved slowly on towards the fatal drop, preceded by the chaplain, the Rev. Mr. Willoughby, and Pilfold Melvin, Esq. The Under-Sheriff; the unhappy convict and the executioner followed, while the officers of the Sheriff, with their wands, brought up the rear. On reaching the drop, the unfortunate man, who still preserved the same firm demeanour which he had from the first exhibited, ascended the platform with a steady and unshaken step, paying the greatest attention to the Rev. Chaplain, who, from the commencement of the awful procession, had been reading the usual service - "I am the resurrection and the life, etc." The culprit having placed himself under the fatal beam, the executioner drew the cap over his face, and while the rope was adjusting, he requested he might endure as little pain as possible, finishing the sentence with these words, "don't hurt me". - Bushby now made several efforts to remove the cap from his mouth, which, being unable to accomplish, the Rev. Chaplain motioned the executioner to remove it for him, which, being complied with, he addressed the people in the following words: - "I hope you will take warning from my fate, and, dear fellows, always attend to the Sabbath day." After a short interval spent in prayer, the drop fell, and the world closed for ever upon the unhappy man, who thus forfeited his life, in the midst of youth, to the offended laws of his country. He appeared to die almost without a struggle. Although Bushby did not… had been executed. There were probably from eight to nine hundred persons present to witness the execution, three parts out of four of whom appeared to be agricultural labourers, who seemed deeply affected at the awful scene, and the most profound silence prevailed amongst them. The Sheriff's javelin men surrounded the gallows and two companies of Foot Guards were drawn up in the square, in the centre of the town, a considerable distance from the gaol and not within sight of the populace. Everything passed off with the utmost order and decorum. After the body had been suspended the usual time, it was cut down and delivered to the friends of the deceased for interment, who were waiting with a cart to receive it."

The presence of a strong military force was a sign of the fear and concern amongst the authorities that things could have got seriously out of control – particularly following the events of November when the troops were also brought in to Horsham.

We will see a little later on that Weslyan Methodism will play a huge part in "teaching the Heathens", and was part of a rising tide of Methodism in Sussex,

Chapter 5: The Swing Riots – *revolt of agricultural labour in the 1830s*

so we can ask, to what extent did the rising tide of Methodism play a part in preventing the unrest becoming a full-scale labouring class revolution[24].

Helevy, in his "England in 1815", thought that Methodism saved England from revolution by diverting the energies of working men and leading them into the paths of responsibility. This sentiment aligns well with the Methodist credo. However, Hobsawm, in his "Labouring Men", published in 1968, doubted whether there were enough Methodists, at the time, to have this effect.

What can be said, with some certainty, is that we have at least one example of a Methodist playing a part in "damping down" a Swing riotous situation. This happened at a riot in Kintbury, Berkshire, where it is reported that "quieting of the labourers was due to the meritorious exertions of Job Hanson, a respectable stonemason and district preacher among the Wesleyan Methodists". So perhaps we can look to the Methodist influence as having a moderating impact, and that being part of the reason for Mannings Heath and Nuthurst not being part of the violent machine breaking and arson that characterised the worst of the Swing Riots.

But there is another, or additional, reason. There are incident reports in parishes all around Nuthurst and Mannings Heath; there were events in Horsham and Cuckfield; mainly threatening letters, riots and gatherings; there was the arson event witnessed by the passengers on the London to Brighton mail coach; and there was an arson event in Rusper on 16th November 1830. In Beeding, Cowfold and Slinfold there were gatherings demanding increases in wages and a reduction in tithes. So, why was nothing reported in Nuthurst or Mannings Heath?

There are references in a number of reports on the riots and labourer hardship, that show some farmers and landowners as being sympathetic to the justice of the labourers demands. There is also evidence of practical sympathy in the parish of Nuthurst, and it took the form of a petition to the House of Commons.

The petition was the work of sixteen Nuthurst "...landowners, tenants and inhabitants... in vestry assembled this 13th day of December, 1831, being liable to the payment of parochial rates...". Hansard records that the petition was presented to the House by Sir Charles Burrell MP *(of Knepp Castle and the MP for the constituency of Shoreham in which Nuthurst, at that time, was to be found)*. Hansard records the petition as being "...from the Landowners of Nuthurst to authorise an equitable adjustment of the able-bodied Labourers upon the Land".

---

24 Socialism, radicalism and nostalgia. Social criticism 1775-1830.

(Unfortunately, we do not have a record of the sixteen signatories to the petition because it was pre. 1834 and, in 1834, Parliament suffered a huge fire in which most of the procedural records, which is where the names would have been recorded, were destroyed.)

The full wording of the petition was published in the Votes and Proceedings of the House of Commons for 17th December 1831, and in the Essex Standard newspaper of 1st January 1832. The thrust of the petition was to bring an end to "the present pernicious and evil system of employing the people *(for practical purposes 'the people' are the agricultural labourers)* in gangs, on parish work, which is disgusting to all good labourers, detrimental to industrious habits, and prejudicial to the morals and character, especially of the younger class of labourers." Strong feelings indeed and a message that was picked up in many agricultural counties. Perhaps the strongest response came from C. Hillyard in an open letter to Parliament, published in the Northampton Mercury of 14th January 1832. He was a prominent Northamptonshire farmer and landowner and wrote a detailed proposal for when, how and by how much, labourers should be paid when out of work in the period between Michaelmas and Lady Day. There are also reports about the Nuthurst petition in the newspapers of the time in many of the Southern Counties, including the Berkshire Chronicle, the Sussex Advertiser, the Hampshire Advertiser, the Brighton Gazette, and it even made the London Evening Standard. So, Nuthurst was well and truly on the national map and attracting a great deal of attention.

The petition is strong evidence that the local landowners and farmers in Nuthurst were very sympathetic to the privations of the labourers and were prepared to act to improve their lot. This, perhaps, explains why the Parish of Nuthurst was free of "Swing" incidents and was taking its own steps to improve the lot of its labourers. The Brighton Gazette was quoted by the London Evening Standard of 1st January 1834, as reporting that: -

"Among the parishes in which the Labourers' Employment Bill has been usefully and beneficially acted upon, may be mentioned Nuthurst and Farnham, in both of which it has, we are informed, been productive of the most advantageous effects. The same has been the case indeed, in various other parishes in different counties, where we have reason to believe that the result has been a greatly increased tranquillity and security of property."

So, little Nuthurst played a real part in improving the lot of the country's agricultural labourers.

Chapter 6

Then Came the Methodists – *arrival in Mannings Heath and the first Chapel and School*

The Methodists arrived in Horsham and Mannings Heath at a time of much civil unrest, where there was resentment amongst the working and labouring classes and a situation where mass action had been shown to yield results. So, indeed, a time of tumult.

The history of Methodism in Horsham is well documented and recorded[25]. The history record shows that the first mention of Methodism in Horsham comes from the diary of John Baker, a wealthy retired lawyer from the West Indies, who rented Park House, in Horsham, in the 1770s. He recorded listening to an itinerant Methodist preacher introduced by Thomas Mann from Petworth. Itinerant preachers were one of the ways the Methodists reached communities, made converts and established places of worship.

However, it was not until the 1820s and 1830s that Methodism really developed in Sussex. Much of this development is attributed to the returning soldiers at the end of the Napoleonic Wars[26]. Many soldiers came from places where John Wesley had been actively preaching in Sussex and making converts: it is highly likely that the soldiers were the catalyst for the growth of Methodism in the South of England.

The end result, in 1832 in Horsham, was that, through the support of Kate Ireland, a Methodist convert, the London Road Wesleyan Methodist Chapel, seating 180 people, was built.

In Mannings Heath, we do not have a well-documented historical record of the events that led, in 1832, to the first Wesleyan Chapel being built. We know that it happened and that it was also used as a school; this is recorded in A History of

---

25 London Road Methodist Church History.
26 The role of soldiers in the origins of Wesleyan Methodism in Sussex.

the County of Sussex[27]. We do not know for sure why Methodism should have taken hold in Mannings Heath – a tiny hamlet of fewer than two hundred souls and fewer than fifty houses, with most of the households headed by agricultural labourers.

So, we must do a little speculating based on the limited records available. The usual springboard for Methodism to take hold in a place was because there was, perhaps, an itinerant preacher visiting who made converts, or perhaps a family of Methodists moved into the area and began to establish a community, or perhaps a marriage happened and the spouse came from a Methodist background.

The Methodist record we do have is in the Brighton Circuit Records[28]. Just as a little explanation – the Methodist church administration is allotted into "Circuits". Circuits are a way of conveniently grouping chapel communities together and, in 1832, both Horsham and Mannings Heath were separate members of the Brighton Circuit, along with a number of Sussex chapels including Rottingdean, Shoreham, Shipley, Hurstpierpoint, Lancing and others. However, by 1841, Mannings Heath and Horsham were being treated as a single entity within the circuit records, making a combined contribution of 11 shillings to the Brighton Circuit.

The 1832 record for Mannings Heath tells us that the Methodist members in Mannings Heath were: -

- John, Mary and Thomas Pronger
- Mary and John Holder
- Edward Chart
- John Potter

These names give us the first clues as to why and how Methodism came to Mannings Heath.

John Holder was not a resident of Mannings Heath in 1832 but genealogical searches indicate that he came from Chichester, was born in 1801 and was married to Mary. The Methodist link is that one of his daughters, Maria, born in 1836 was christened at the Chichester Wesleyan chapel of St Pancras. Perhaps he was the itinerant preacher? We will never know for sure, but the Methodist/Wesleyan link to him is clearly there.

---

27 A History of the County of Sussex, Volume 6.
28 Brighton Circuit Methodist Records.

Chapter 6: Then Came the Methodists – *arrival in Mannings Heath*

The name of Chart was well known in the Parish of Nuthurst and in Horsham. It is a name that will occur throughout this story and, because of their importance, the genealogy of the Chart family from the 1770s to the 1900s is included as Appendix 1.

We do not know for sure whether the Edward Chart in ref. 28 is the Edward Chart born in 1783 and originally from Worth, or the Edward Chart born in 1813 and from Nuthurst. I suspect it was the former, who would have been 39 years old in 1832 and an established farmer at Great Ventors in Monks Gate, whereas the latter would have been a young man of just 19. We do not know, but we do know something of the Methodist link.

William Chart from Ifield married a Sarah Tullet in 1812. The Non-Conformist Record Indexes show a large number of Sussex Tullet family members as being Methodists, and it may well be that it was Sarah who was the catalyst for the Charts becoming staunch members of the Methodists with Amos, of whom we shall hear more of later in the story, being a leading light in Methodism in Horsham and in Mannings Heath.

John Potter was born in 1789 in Horsham and, at the time of opening the Methodist Chapel, he was living with his wife Jane and two daughters, at Bulls Cottage, Sedgwick. His links with Methodism are clear; he was baptised in the Horsham Non-Conformist Chapel (that operated from 1784 to 1800) by George Gilbert, the Protestant Dissenting Minister, on 6th June 1789[29].

The Prongers were Mannings Heath farmers and, whilst there is no direct link between this family and Protestant Dissent, there may well be family links between the Mannings Heath Prongers and their Dissenting or Methodist relations in other Sussex villages.

In addition, comparison of the 1841 census with the non-Conformist records of births, marriages and deaths shows that many Mannings Heath family names were common in Sussex Methodism in the mid-18th century to the early 19th century. Weller, Wickens, Jupp, Funnell, Waller, Woolven and Wisden are primary examples. Whilst this does not prove a strong Methodist presence in Mannings Heath in 1832, it certainly suggests a significant non-conformist presence, and some will undoubtedly have had Methodist "leanings" if not formal membership of that church.

So, we have speculated on the basis for the beginnings of the Methodist congregation in Mannings Heath – what else do we know?

---

29 Register of Births and Baptisms.

We know where they built their Wesleyan Chapel and School because it is shown on the 1841 Tithe Map in Chapter 3. We can also pinpoint it even more closely from two sources: -

1. "Memories of Mannings Heath"[30] in which Felix Thorns recalls his father showing him the footings of an old building which had been, he said, the "old" school. These footings were described as being about 50 yards from what is now the entrance to Gaggle Wood, towards the School House and the Common. Felix was born in 1909, so this childhood memory could have been in about 1917, and his father would have been around in Mannings Heath when the Chapel was still standing.
2. The National Archives contain documents relating to schools in Nuthurst[31]. One of these documents identifies the position of the 1832 Chapel and school as being "about 80 yards" from the Recreation (Public) Ground that is now known as the Common.

Taking these items of information, and what is shown on the 1841 Tithe Map in Chapter 3, gives us a location for the Chapel, as shown below, when superimposed on today's Mannings Heath.

1832 location of the Methodist Chapel and School at what is now the entrance to the Timbers housing estate

And we know more – ref. 31 also contains a plan and elevation drawing of the school produced in 1882 to support a case for this building to become the Board

---

30 Memories of Mannings Heath – memories of past times in the West Sussex village of Mannings Heath.
31 Elementary Education Parish Files – Nuthurst. National Archives ED2/442.

school following the 1870 Education Act - but more of that later. It was a very simple building, 42 feet long and 15 feet 6 inches wide, with boys' and girls' toilets at the end away from the door, which faced on to Golding Lane, and it was equipped with a stove. We know from later records that it was able to house around sixty pupils, when used as a school.

One other significant unknown is where the money came from to build the Chapel. Money for the Horsham Chapel came from, among others, Kate Ireland, but we have no record of similar Mannings Heath benefactors.

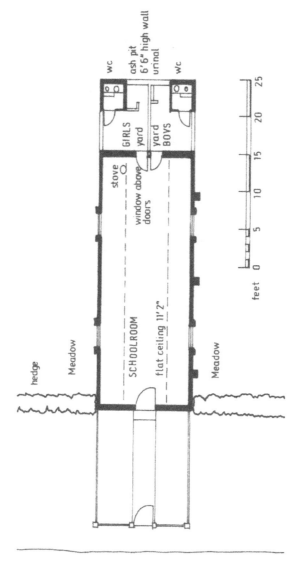

Plan of the chapel and school in 1832.
Prepared from information contained in Ref. 31.

The building is likely to have cost about £200 to build in 1832. Relative to earnings, this was a substantial sum, being over four times the annual earnings of an agricultural labourer.

And this is what the Chapel and School may have looked like in 1832.

[The plan drawing and the impression of what the chapel and school building would have looked like were created from the information in Ref.31 by John Fortune B. Arch DipTP RIBA of Nuthurst, West Sussex.]

Chapter 7

1832, The First School – *the beginnings of "Teaching the Heathens"*

Raymond Williams, who is recognised as one of the most perceptive and influential thinkers of the mid 1900s, recorded this quotation, by a Justice of the Peace, in his "Long Revolution"[32]:-

"It is doubtless desirable that the poor should be generally instructed in reading, if it were only for the best purposes – that they may read the Scriptures. As to writing and arithmetic, it may be apprehended that such a degree of knowledge would produce in them a disrelish for the laborious occupations of life."

These words reflect the views of the upper classes, often expressed in Parliament and elsewhere, at a time when civil unrest was in the air and the "ruling classes" were nervous about the labouring classes acquiring knowledge and access to information that could further foment unrest.

The level of poverty among the labouring classes, and the reliance on the income brought in to the family from the work of the children, meant that there was a real reluctance to give up those earnings for the possible benefits of time spent on their education[33]. Employment of children continued to increase into the latter half of the century.

---

32 The Long Revolution.
33 The History of Education in England in the Nineteenth Century.

The Rev. Jabez Bunting (1779-1858) was one of the foremost Methodist preachers and thinkers recognised by many as the heir to John Wesley. He became President of the first Wesleyan theological college and the educational standard of Wesleyan ministers and the congregation of Methodists was a primary concern of his.

G.M. Best has written widely on Methodist history and quotes Jabez Bunting as saying[34]:-

"Education... Without religion is not education. I think that an education which looks only at the secular interests of an individual, which looks only at his condition as a member of civil society, and does not look upon him as a man having an immortal soul... is not education."

Reference 3, and in particular the Rector's observations quoted in Chapter 3, make clear that, at least in his view, the poor, labouring class were desirous of education and schooling.

This is just a sample of the conflicting thoughts, attitudes and ideas on education that were swirling around in the early part of the 19th century.

The hard economic need for children to work and the underpinning desire in the labouring classes to become better educated as part of a route out of poverty,

---

[34] A Historical Perspective.

Chapter 7: 1832, The First School – *the beginnings of "Teaching the Heathens"*

created a natural environment for the establishment of Sunday schools, which would enable education to take place at a time that still allowed children to work and earn on the other six days of the week.

Robert Raikes (1735-1811) was editor of the Gloucester Journal and generally recognised as the founder of the Sunday School movement in England. He met with John Wesley and they shared views on the need to educate the children of the poor. It was Robert Raikes who said: -

"The world marches forth on the feet of little children."

The first Sunday school in England opened in 1751 in Nottingham[35]. A later school was opened by a friend of John Wesley, named Hannah Ball, in High Wycombe. But it was the work of Robert Raikes that gave impetus to the whole movement. He opened his first Sunday school in Gloucester in 1781, and just four years later there were 250,000 children going to Sunday school, with numbers continuing to grow at an increasing rate. By 1818, there were nearly half a million scholars, by 1833 there were 1.5 million, and by 1851 there were nearly 2.5 million, which represented one in seven of the child population of England[36].

All of this history supports the contention that the Mannings Heath School in the Methodist Chapel started as a Sunday School, and we do have a specific reference to support this.

---

35 Sunday School- Wikipedia.
36 Victorian Childhood – Themes and Variations.

Reference 30 contains recollections of Mannings Heath recorded by Mrs Flint. She wrote: -

"The first Methodist church was started in the village 130 years ago. [This dates Mrs Flint's recollections to having been written in 1960-1970.] *I remember my grandfather, Mr Worcester, who lived in Nuthurst was Sunday School*

Superintendent and he would walk to Mannings Heath every Sunday morning to Sunday school with his two youngest children, bringing their dinner with them and staying for afternoon Sunday School and service before walking back to Nuthurst for tea."

Research of the census and birth records suggests that the "grandfather" to whom Mrs Flint is referring is Walter Worcester, who was born in 1827 and lived for most of his life in Nuthurst. He had five children and their ages suggests that her grandfather's walks to Mannings Heath were probably before she was born, or at least at a time when she would have been too young to have a first-hand memory. Not unusually in this sort of memory recall, the re-caller is, in fact, "remembering" something described to them rather than actually witnessing it first-hand.

So, what was school like?

Shortly after the chapel was built, Mannings Heath and Horsham left the Brighton Circuit and both became members of the Dorking and Horsham Methodist Circuit. Other members of the circuit included Southwater, Rudgwick, Haven, Five Oaks, Capel and Hammer. We have the Preaching Plans[37] and they tell us that a service took place in the Mannings Heath chapel every Sunday at 2.30pm. The preachers were busy folk because, very often, the same preacher took services in Horsham at 10.30am and 6.30pm as well as the 2.30pm service in Mannings Heath.

We know, then, that at least an hour of the Sunday afternoon was taken up with a service. Ref. 33 contains a "typical" timetable for a Sunday School in Oldham. Fitting that around the chapel service gives us a timetable like this, using the same "phrasing" as in the original: -

---

[37] Plan of the Wesleyan Methodist Preachers.

Chapter 7: 1832, The First School – *the beginnings of "Teaching the Heathens"*

Time	Order	Time Allowed	Time of Ceasing
½ past 9.	Call Registers.	5 min.	20m. past 9.
20m. past 9.	Singing and Prayer.	15 min.	25 m. to 10.
25 m. to 10.	The appointed lesson that has been perfectly committed to memory; and also, if time permits, some additional reading.	30 min.	5 m. past 10.
5 m. past 10.	Call Registers. Classes prepare for Chapel.	15 min.	20 m. past 10.
20 m. past 10.	Singing and Reading Lesson, with questions and explanations: if time permits, Catechism or a Spelling Lesson to be introduced.	60 min.	20 m. past 11.
20 m. past 11.	Singing and a short Address from the Superintendent.	25 m.	15 min. to 12.
15 min. to 12.	Singing and Prayer.	15 min.	12 o'clock.
	Pupils home for lunch.		
2 o'clock	Call Registers.	5 min.	5 m. past 2.
5 m. past 2.	Singing and Prayer.	10 min.	15 m. past 2.
15 m. past 2.	Call Registers. Classes prepare for Chapel.	15 min.	30 m. past 2.
30 m. past 2.	Chapel Service led by the visiting Preacher.	60 min.	30 m. past 3.
30 m. past 3.	Reading Lesson, with questions and explanations; and, if time permits, a little Catechism.	30 min.	4 o'clock
4 o'clock	Spelling or an interesting story; singing and Prayer. Depart for home.	30 min.	30 m. past 4

This time table follows closely on the tenets of Jabez Bunting and Robert Raikes by teaching the children to read using the bible and catechism. As the Sunday school movement grew, so did the breadth of the curriculum until the second half of the 19th century, when teaching embraced the "three Rs" and made use of texts other than the bible.

What a typical Victorian Sunday school class room might have looked like.

The methods of teaching relied heavily on repetition and the "monitorial" system[38].

Examples of the repetition style of teaching were: -

- chanting of tables;
- repetitious copying of what the teacher had written on the blackboard; and
- learning and recitation of verse and prose passages.

The "monitorial" system used the older and abler pupils to teach the younger and less able, thus enabling one teacher to cope with a large class.

---

[38] Education in England: a brief history (Chapter 2).

Chapter 8

A Ferment of Activity – *towards compulsory universal education*

Leaving our Mannings Heath Sunday School for a little while, we need to look at the "bigger scene" to put the next stages of "teaching the Heathens" into context.

The 19th century saw a constant stream of political initiatives on both local and national scales, all leading towards compulsory elementary education. There was a growing awareness that things needed to change. There was pressure from industry to have a better educated workforce to compete with our European rivals, and there was societal pressure, from the lower classes in particular, to better themselves: they saw education as a route out of abject poverty.

Some of the key dates in this 19th century "ferment" are[39]:-

1811	National Society	Founded by the Church of England with the declared intention of putting a church school in every parish. By 1851, it had 12,000 schools across England and Wales.
1832	Representation of the People Act	Known as the Reform Act and gave voting rights to small landowners, tenant farmers, shopkeepers and house holders paying more than £10 per year in rent. Created 67 new constituencies and got rid of 56 "rotten boroughs". Thought to be a direct response of Parliament to the unrest and riots of 1830. Estimated to have given the vote to a million more people.

---

39 Education in England Timeline.

1836	Methodist Conference	Methodists decided to start the creation of weekday schools. The determination was "What we wish for is not merely schools but Church schools... Not merely education but education which may begin in infant school and end in Heaven".
1839	Committee of the Privy Council on Education established	Placed education at the highest level of government and directly under the eye of the Monarch. This was the beginning of the state contributing to the funding of education by distributing a grant of £20,000 per year.
1840	Grammar Schools Act	Made it lawful for grammar schools to apply their income, usually from long-standing endowments, to the teaching of subjects other than the classics and classical languages. This was an attempt to raise the standards of more "commercial" subjects.
1841	School Sites Acts	Five Acts, between 1841 and 1852, that facilitated the purchase of land for schools and for the making of "Parliamentary Grants for the Education of the Poor".
1847	Government Grants	Annual grants started being made, by the Government, to Wesleyan Methodist schools and the Catholic Poor School Committee.
1848	Woodard Society	An Anglican charitable trust providing Anglican boarding schools. Lancing College, Hurstpierpoint and Ardingly College are three of the current Woodard Trust schools. Canon Nathaniel Woodard (1811-1891) was born in Shoreham, his aim was to provide education founded on "sound principle and sound knowledge, firmly grounded in the Christian faith".
1854	Literary and Scientific Institutions Act	Facilitated the establishment of institutions for the promotion of literature, science and the arts. This 160-year-old Act has become a legal vehicle for today's protestors trying to prevent Councils closing libraries as a means of making economies.
1861	Newcastle Report	Report of the "Royal Commission on the state of popular education in England". This report laid the ground for, and led the way to, the 1870 Elementary Education Act.

Chapter 8: A Ferment of Activity – *towards compulsory universal education*

1870	Elementary Education Act[40]	Drafted by Liberal MP William Forster and also known as the Forster Act. The act opens with, "There shall be provided for every school district a sufficient amount of accommodation in public elementary schools… available for all the children resident in such district…"

As a result of the 1870 Act, 2,500 new school boards were created that were independent of existing local government. Education was neither free (except for proven poverty) nor was it compulsory.

Returning to Mannings Heath – 1869 and 1870 were turning points in the story of teaching the Heathens and the story continues to unfold with the building of the second Wesleyan Methodist Chapel in Golding Lane in 1869.

---

40 Education in England (Chapter 3)

Chapter 9

1869: The Second Chapel – *and the beginnings of the Wesleyan/Methodist Elementary School*

The second chapel is shown on the 1897 Ordnance Survey map, along with the first chapel, the Mannings Heath C.E. School, which opened in 1883, and the School House that provided accommodation for a number of the school head teachers.

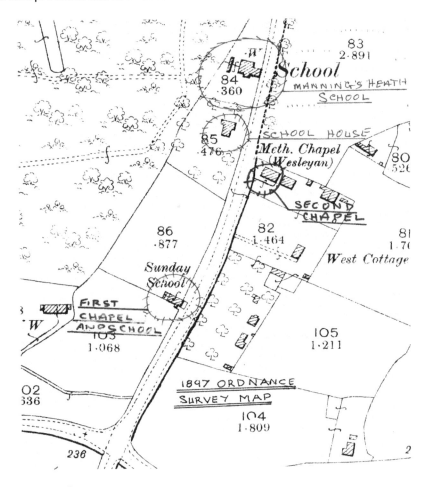

1897 Ordnance Survey

First Chapel built 1832. Second Chapel built 1869. Mannings Heath School built 1883. School House built 1890.

Chapter 9: 1869: The Second Chapel

The building of the second chapel has an important part to play in the story of "teaching the Heathens". Firstly, it allowed the first Chapel to be converted into a full five-day school from its earlier role as a Sunday school. Secondly, it introduces us to Amos chart, who was one of the main "driving forces" behind the building of the second Chapel and the use of the first chapel as a "proper" five-day school, as well as promoting it as a viable alternative to the building of a brand-new CE/Board school in response to the 1870 Act. We will get to know Amos a little better in a while.

The story of the opening of the second chapel is fully reported in Albery's Monthly Illustrated Journal for September 1869[41].

The report refers to the building of a "small chapel" in 1832 and this is the first chapel described, and illustrated in Chapter 6. It goes on to refer to the "opposition" to Methodism both in Horsham and in Mannings Heath, with the resulting decline in membership. However, it does tell us of a "remnant of faithful ones" driving a revival, resulting in the first chapel becoming too small. It is worth noting that the 1851 Ecclesiastical Census[42] shows almost as many attendees at the "small" Mannings Heath Chapel as at the main Nuthurst Parish Church of St Andrew's, so perhaps the first chapel really was becoming too small.

In ref. 25, Sue Checkland et al., confirm this "revival" and that the 1860s brought "new zeal and enthusiasm". This was supported by the involvement of the Cramp and Chart families and, in the latter case, driven forward by Amos Chart. Ref. 25 also tells us about the "ring of chapels", including Mannings Heath, constructed using the Horsham congregation initiatives and finance. This is confirmed in Albery's report, referring to the "untiring energies of Rev. C.O. Eldrige and his flock" of subscribers and friends.

---

41 Opening of the New Wesleyan Chapel at Mannings Heath. Albery's Sept. 1869.
42 Horsham Ecclesiastical Census Returns (1851).

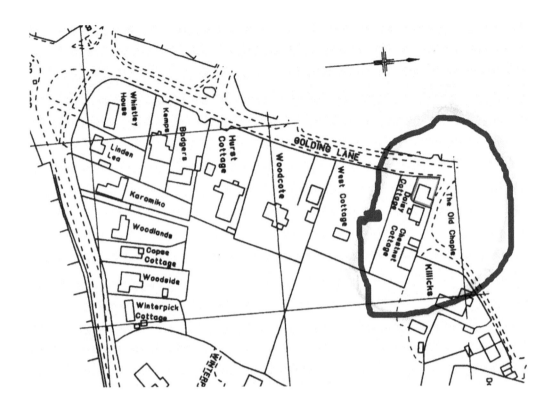

Amongst the Mannings Heath Methodists were the Wickens family. Alan Flint, in ref. 30, tells us that one of the Wickens family sold the piece of land for the chapel for the sum of £5. More detail of this transaction and subsequent chapel history is given by H. Browning, the great grandson of Thomas Wickens, who sold the plot of land[43]. Thomas was the owner of Chestnut Cottage and bought the adjoining piece of land from the Enclosure Commissioner on which to build another cottage (Daisy Cottage). It was a small piece of this second plot that Thomas sold to the Methodist Church trustees to build their second chapel.

The Chapel was built by a Mr Potter of Horsham and, remarkably by today's standards, construction commenced in the Spring of 1869 with the memorial stone laid on 24th June, and the whole building completed and formally opened on 19th August of the same year – no more than six months from start to finish.

The opening ceremony lasted all day, with a sermon in the morning and another in the afternoon, and was attended by the "great and the good" of the Methodist circuits from Redhill, Horsham, Cowfold, Dorking, Reigate and Ockley; so, it was seen as a very significant event in the life of Methodism in the Horsham area.

---

43 "Serving both God and Mammon" WSCT June 1973.

Chapter 9: 1869: The Second Chapel 49

Albery's report also tells us that "The old Chapel *[the First Chapel then being used as a Sunday School]* is now to be converted into a school room". This tidily closes the link between the second Methodist Chapel and the story of "teaching the Heathens".

Mr Browning (in ref. 43) also tells us that, by 1972, the Methodist numbers had dropped to a point where the trustees decided to cease the chapel functioning as a place of worship on 7th May 1972, and to apply to the Horsham Rural District Council for a change of use to a domestic dwelling. This change ultimately came about in 1973 and the chapel was sold for £9,500[44].

The "new" (second) Chapel in about 1870. It is now known as the "Old Chapel".

The bearded gentleman, second from the left, looks remarkably like Amos Chart.

---

44 Minute Book of the Trustees.

The second Chapel, as it is today (2016) as a private dwelling. For a building, constructed in under six months nearly 150 years ago, it is looking remarkably fine.

Amos Chart was a well-known "character" in the Horsham community, in local Methodism and was important in the Methodist community in Mannings Heath, both in the affairs of the chapels and, as we will see later in the story, in "teaching the Heathens" both in the first chapel school and the moves to create the C.E./Board school which came into being in 1883.

So, this is an appropriate point in the story to get to know a little more about Amos, who is shown on the Chart family genealogy in Appendix 1.

He was born in 1837 at Great Venters farm and was the oldest of four children to Edward and Emily. His father died in 1862 and the 1871 census shows Amos as head of the household and farming Venters at 100 acres and employing three farm labourers; clearly a man of substance at 36 years of age. In 1864, he married Mary Ann Stone, from Nuthurst, at St Andrew's Church, Nuthurst. They had four sons – George, Fred, Amos and John, the youngest, born in 1871. Mary died in 1879 at the tender age of only 44, leaving Amos as a widower.

Chapter 9: 1869: The Second Chapel

On 3rd August 1881, the 44-year-old Amos married 22-year-old Ellen Ellis in the Congregational Chapel, Burgess Hill. She was the daughter of Thomas and Rebecca, who had a shop and estate agency in Burgess Hill. She and Amos had five children, Olive, Ernest, Arthur, Herbert and Percy, the youngest, born in 1898, when Amos was 61. In the parish of Nuthurst, Amos had careers as a farmer and, latterly, as the local road surveyor. In 1890, he and Ellen, and their children, moved into Horsham where Amos became the proprietor of a merchandising business located at the junction of East Street and Park Street. He dealt in hay, corn, straw, coal and coke, gravel, lime and manure, bread, flour, firewood, linseed, birdseed, oatmeal and garden seeds[45]. He also became the Horsham Sub-Postmaster. Clearly a man of many parts.

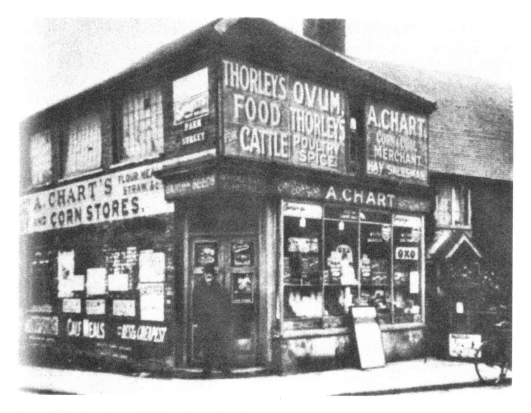

Amos Chart's shop with East St. to the right and Park St. to the left. The photograph was taken in about 1909 when Amos was 72. The white-bearded man in the doorway is thought to be Amos.

Amos died in 1919 at the age of 82 and was much respected for his honesty and acumen. He was executor for the estates of a number of friends and relatives,

---

45 Photo history-Sussex reprinted from Kelly's Directory.

including the brother of his first wife, his mother, Emily, his friend and colleague Simeon Comber and for Emily Tyrell[46].

Amos made a significant contribution to Methodist life in Mannings Heath and Horsham and to the school in Mannings Heath.

In the period between 1870 and 1883, there was much discussion and correspondence about the "new" C.E./Board school proposed for Mannings Heath. In Chapter 5, I describe the beginnings of Methodism in Mannings Heath and the first chapel. On 28th June 1881, Amos Chart, in his capacity as Chairman of the Methodist school based in the first chapel, intervened in the discussions and correspondence, by writing to the Local Education Authority with a proposal that the existing Methodist School should become the "official" Mannings Heath school, avoiding the need to build a new school[47]. This "stirred the pot" and is discussed in more detail later on, but it was a move of some courage on the part of the Methodists. The proposal was ultimately rejected by the Local Education Authority after they carried out an inspection of the first chapel school.

In 1892, Amos was confirmed as the Leader of the Mannings Heath Methodists[48]. In 1894 he led the Valediction of the Rev. C.M. Greenway at his farewell service and address in the Horsham Methodist Chapel and, in 1895, he was made a Trustee of the Mannings Heath and Horsham Methodist Chapels[49].

In 1894, Amos was a candidate for election in the new Horsham Urban District Council.

---

46 Probate Calendar of England and Wales.
47 National Archives. Nuthurst Parish Files. ED2/442.
48 Horsham and Dorking Circuit Schedule Book.
49 Horsham and Mannings Heath Methodist records.

Chapter 9: 1869: The Second Chapel

HORSHAM URBAN DISTRICT COUNCIL

TO THE ELECTORS.

LADIES AND GENTLEMEN,

At the request of a number of ratepayers, I have been induced to come forward as a Candidate for the Horsham District Council.

Whilst feeling unworthy of the honour of this post, yet I deem it my duty, as a citizen, to do what I can for the welfare of the town with which I have been acquainted all my life, and where I have now resided for over eleven years.

I have in various ways had experience in parish matters, and for several years filled the post of Road Surveyor in the Parish of Nuthurst, so have a practical acquaintance with many of these matters that will come under the consideration of the Council.

I do not offer myself in connection with any political party, as, in my opinion, the affairs of the District Council ought to be wholly disconnected with politics.

It will be my endeavour, if elected, to secure for the Town good sanitary arrangements, a good supply of pure water, good dwellings for the poor, and providing allotments for working men, should they wish it.

Thanking you in anticipation for your kind support,

I am, Ladies and Gentlemen,
Your Obedient Servant,

AMOS CHART.

39, NORTH STREET & 48, PARK STREET,
HORSHAM, November 29th, 1894.

Amos Chart's election address to the electors of Horsham. Thirty-five people put themselves forward for election for fifteen places. Unfortunately, Amos, with 432 votes was 16th, so was not elected.

In 1904, ref 46 tells us that Amos Chart was Trustee and Leader of the Mannings Heath School Room in the first chapel. This is interesting because it shows that the building was still there in 1904 and was still in use as a school, but only as a premises for a Sunday School. However, the life of the building was limited and between 1909 and 1911, Amos was charged with the disposal of the site of the first chapel and, as it had become, Sunday school[50]. Ultimately, the site was sold to Mr Scrase Dickins for £2 in 1911.

---

50 Horsham and Dorking Circuit Records.

Amos Chart in later life; possibly in about 1910. The picture does explain why ref. 43 contains the statement that "Amos Chart was regarded as a local character in Horsham". He was known as "Father Chart" by Horsham children and sometimes they mistakenly thought that the Lord's Prayer said "Our Father Chart in Heaven"!

The Sussex County Times, in January 1919, recorded the death of Amos and gave him a fulsome obituary. It recorded his long-time support for, and action within, the "Wesleyan/Methodist Connection", his lifetime as a staunch Liberal and Temperance Association supporter, along with his friend and fellow Horsham business man, Jury Cramp, who was one of the mourners at the funeral service at the London Road Methodist Chapel and the interment in Hills Cemetery.

Chapter 10

1870 – The Wesleyan/Methodist Elementary School - *and the emergence of William Reading*

As we shall see, the school was led by William Reading, as its teacher, and became known as "Readings" school, so, for simplicity, it will be referred to as that from hence.

Ref. 31 contains a document, prepared by Amos Chart in his capacity as trustee of the "Mannings Heath Wesleyan School", that is the Preliminary Statement of details of the Readings school. The National Archives original document is in a damaged state, but the main points from it are as follows: -

- The school was governed by a committee acting under a deed *(presumably as put in place by the Wesleyan/Methodist Trustees led by Amos Chart).*
- It was classed as an "Adventure School" meaning that it was conducted by the teacher at his own risk and his responsibility. *(This means that it did not come under the inspection of the Education Authority and did not receive any grant or subsidy).*
- The building belonged to The Wesleyan Society without any occupation fee.
- It was reported as being a school for fifty-four pupils (twenty boys, sixteen girls and eighteen infants).
- The building (the first chapel) was built in 1832 and it became established as a school in 1870. *(See Chapter 6)*
- The annual income for the school was £18 19s for 1881, made up of a £5 "voluntary contribution" *(presumably from the Methodist Chapel congregation)* and £13 19s from school fees. *(This fee income amounts to a payment of about 2 ½ d per week from each pupil).*
- William Reading is stated to be the Master and his birth-date is given as 17th June 1852. His start date in the position of Master is given as April 1870. This ties in with the date of the opening of the second chapel in 1869 and the report that the first chapel was to be converted into a school. *(It is interesting to note that William Reading became the Master of a school of some fifty pupils when he was two months short of his 18th birthday. He must have been a person of some real substance – firstly to have the self-confidence*

to take on the challenge and secondly to have gained the confidence of the Trustees that he could do the job).

- It is recorded that William was not a qualified, certificated teacher but was willing to be assessed, and Amos Chart gave the opinion that he would be a candidate for a certificate under articles.
- As well as teaching, William is recorded as having a Saturday job as a book keeper with an income of £12 per annum from that work.
- It is likely that William had at least one assistant because the girls are reported as being taught needlework as part of their curriculum.
- It is recorded that the school will "be conducted as a Public Elementary School within the meaning of the 1870 Elementary Education Act".
- It is confirmed that the school does not lie within a "District for which a School Board has been formed".

The School Board for Mannings Heath did not come into being until the Mannings Heath C.E./Board school was built in 1883, and it was the last two bullet points above that created the opportunity for Amos Chart and the Methodists to propose that Readings should become the "official" elementary school for Mannings Heath.

So, what of the education in Readings School?

Unfortunately, there are none of the normal school records – such as the Teacher's Log Books, Trustee meeting minutes etc. - still in existence in any of the record repositories such as the County Record Offices and the National Archives. So, we have to draw on other sources.

Firstly, the premises; we know that it had a floor area of about 500 ft^2. If we take out an area for a teacher's desk, blackboard and book/equipment storage, we are left with an area of about 400 ft^2 for the fifty to sixty pupils. This gives a space of about 2ft 6ins x 2ft 6ins for each pupil. This would have been a very crowded space, difficult to move around and difficult to separate pupils into different working groups. It would have been totally unacceptable by today's standards both on education and safety grounds. As we shall see later, when describing the creation of the C.E./Board school, this space consideration had much to do with why Amos did not succeed in winning acceptance of Readings as the "official" elementary school for Mannings Heath.

Chapter 10: 1870 – The Wesleyan/Methodist Elementary School

This is a picture of a "typical" Victorian elementary school class room and Readings would have been similar to this, certainly in terms of its congestion.

What of the education standards? When the 1870 Act came into effect, so did school boards, education authorities etc., with the associated administrative requirements and educational standards. The New Code of 1879 contained the "Standards of Examination". There will be more on this when we come to the C.E./Board school later but, for now, I will use the Standards for writing as a means of looking at results from Readings[51].

Standard	Requirements
1	Copy a line of print, on slates or in copy books, at choice of managers; and write from dictation a few common words.
2	A sentence from the same book slowly read once, and then dictated. Copy books (large or half-text) to be shown.
3	A sentence slowly dictated once from the same book. Copy books to be shown (small hand, capital letters, and figures).
4	Eight lines slowly dictated once from a reading book. Copy books to be shown (improved small hand).

---

51 Scholars and Slates – Sussex Schools in the 1880s.

Standard	Requirements
5	Writing from memory the substance of a short story read out twice; spelling, grammar and handwriting to be considered.
6	A short theme or letter; the composition, spelling, grammar and handwriting to be considered.

We have a record of the standards achieved in Readings because we know the pupils who transferred to the C.E./Board school in 1883/4 from Readings[52] and these records are transcribed in Appendix 2.

The results show that the 12-, 13- and 14-year-olds, who may have been under William Reading's tutelage for seven to nine years, have mostly reached level 4, with just three falling below this standard. As a comparison, the C.E./Board school was achieving Standard 4 for most of its 11- and 12-year-old pupils in the mid-1930s. So, taking into account all the circumstances that advantaged the later school, it is fair to say that William Reading, in the 1870s, was doing a very good job of teaching the Heathens.

Now we need to get to know William Reading a little better. He was the teacher in charge of the Methodist School (Readings) and continued as a teacher in the C.E./Board school that came into being in 1883.

William was born in 1852 and was the third of the four children of Robert and Emily Reading.

Robert was, to say the least, a colourful character. He was born in 1813 in Effingham, Surrey.

---

[52] Mannings Heath School Register of Admissions.

Chapter 10: 1870 – The Wesleyan/Methodist Elementary School

Robert Reading 1813-1911

Picture reproduced from reference 53 with the permission of the Southwater Local History Group.

He came to Horsham in 1833 and took part in horse races in St Leonards Forest where, racing under the Bazalgette colours, he was also employed as a manservant to a lawyer, Henry Padwick, in Horsham's Carfax[53]. By 1851, just a year before William was born, he became an inn keeper, becoming landlord of the Punchbowl in Middle Street, Horsham, and this is probably where William was born in 1852. By 1861, Robert had become the innkeeper at the Dun Horse in Mannings Heath. At that time, the Dun Horse would have looked much as shown in the photograph in Chapter 3.

We know William attended the St Andrew's elementary school in Nuthurst – the school log book records him as being there in 1863 when he would have been 11 years old[54]. Later on, he attended Mr Baxter's private school, adjacent to

---

53 Southwater Victorians – Lives and Portraits.
54 Kathleen Langley notes.

the Bedford Hotel, in Station Road, Horsham. In 1864, at the age of 12, he contracted rheumatic fever, which left him partially crippled for the rest of his life.

William Reading

Picture reproduced from reference 53 with the permission of the Southwater Local History Group.

Readings School opened its doors on 10th January 1870, and, as described earlier, it continued with William as the teacher and de-facto "Head", as the only school in Mannings Heath up until the C.E./Board school opened in 1883.

As well as his teaching, William was at the heart of much that went on in Mannings Heath right up to his death in 1937. A pen-picture of William in the Mannings Heath community, and particularly his contribution to the Nuthurst Cricket Club has been written by another local historian, David Boorman[55].

William was secretary and treasurer of the cricket club from 1886 until at least 1913, and continued as a "servant" of the club into the 1930s – 60 years' service for which he was presented with an illuminated address by the members in April 1931. He is quoted as saying, "They knew I couldn't run *(due to the rheumatic fever he contracted as a child, that left him disabled),* so they allowed me to become treasurer".

---

55 The Nutters – a history.

Chapter 10: 1870 – The Wesleyan/Methodist Elementary School

In the West Sussex County Times of 11th April 1931, there is a report of William's "reminiscences" of his life in Mannings Heath and, in particular, his time with the "Nutters" Cricket Club. One of the little "gems" is William's story about a certain umpire; he very much resembled, William said, the fat boy of the "Pickwick Papers". In one particular match, the batsman had duly "taken centre" and, after he had been batting for some time, his wicket was spread-eagled. "How's that," the shout went up. "A little more to the leg I said," was the umpire's response because, as William said, his "active thought" had ceased with the first over.

There are many references to his interest in village activities and, for many years, he was the driving force behind the Working Men's' Club that met in the old "Drill" Hall, next to the school built in 1883, in Golding Lane.

He was totally committed to his role as the Readings teacher and so, when moves to replace his school with a C.E./Board school under the local Education Authority began, he was much disturbed for his own future and that of his charges.

The first murmurings of a new school in Mannings Heath are recorded[56] as surfacing in 1872, only a couple of years after the opening of Readings school, but doubtless the beginnings of the Parish of Nuthurst having to respond to the 1870 Education Act. Ref. 56 is a diary of Mrs Augusta Bigg: the Bigg family were the owners of the Swallowfield estate and a leading Mannings Heath family. Their history, and place in the life of Mannings Heath is documented in "The Story of Swallowfield" by Tony Turner[57].

---

56 Mrs Augusta Bigg's Diaries 1872-1875.
57 The Story of Swallowfield.

Augusta Bigg. Wife of Smith Henry Bigg of Swallowfield, Mannings Heath and mother of Augusta (see below). Further information in ref. 57.

Born 1810, London. Died 1888, at Swallowfield.

On 6th December 1872, Augusta records that Mr McCarogher *(the Nuthurst Parish Rector)* "…brought the plans of the new school which is to be on the Common here. Mr Hurst asked £50 for the ground, Major Aldridge gave the stone, Mr Blew has drawn the plans". In 1873, funds are beginning to be raised and, on 26th February, Augusta records that "There was a meeting at the Dun Horse yesterday to fix on the site for the new school". At the time, William's family were the Dun Horse innkeepers and William was living there, so he must have been aware of what was afoot.

On 11th February 1873, Augusta records that "There has been a great stir in the Parish about the Chapel School on the common. *(This was Readings School and was, in fact, not on the Common but on the opposite side of Golding Lane, as described in Chapters 6 and 9.)* Mr McCarogher having had several letters from "the Education Department" to say it must be done away with, not being efficient. Henry *(Henry Bigg, her husband)* says we have no power to put it

Chapter 10: 1870 – The Wesleyan/Methodist Elementary School

down, being a private school. Chart *(almost certainly a reference to Amos Chart)* has had copies of the letters to show their *(the Methodists) Superintendent*". There is more about the Education Department inspection of, and views on, the Readings school in the later chapters discussing the beginnings of the C.E./Board school in 1883, but the evidence of the standards attained by William's pupils gives a clear picture of a school that must have been far better than the words "not being efficient" imply.

Things seem to have quietened until the Autumn of 1882 when Augusta's daughter, also Augusta, becomes involved in events concerning the new Mannings Heath school[58] and also with William and the Readings school. Augusta met William and, from her diary entry for 14th September 1882, is clearly concerned that William may not be able to continue as a teacher should a C.E./Board school come into being. William's fear is probably because he was never a qualified, certificated teacher, despite his excellent teaching and leadership work with the Readings school.

Augusta Bigg (the daughter) of Swallowfield, Mannings Heath.
Her diaries show she was a supporter of William Reading and his work as a teacher.

She was born in Hampstead in 1836 and died at Ryecroft in Mannings Heath in 1922.

---

58 Miss Augusta Bigg's Diaries 1880-1884.

Augusta clearly thinks highly of William and his work, and that shines through in many of her diary entries leading up to 21st January 1884, when the transfer of pupils from Readings to the new C.E./Board school took place and, after a meeting with the Head Teacher of the new school, William was taken on as assistant master. This must have been a huge personal relief for him on two counts. Firstly, his ability to continue in his chosen profession, and secondly, his ability to continue to work with his Readings pupils.

A further piece of evidence of the high regard in which Augusta held William is recorded in her will. She made a specific bequest of an income of £26 per annum to William in 1922.

The next big change in William's affairs happened after he had been teaching in Mannings Heath school for three years and was 35 years of age. Louisa Buck arrived as the new Head Teacher in September 1885 (see Appendix 3). Louisa was 36 years old and had been born in Silverton, Devon. She was the daughter of an Inland Revenue Officer and came to the Mannings Heath school from a teaching position in Honiton, Devon[59], so Mannings Heath was a promotion for her as a qualified and certificated Elementary Teacher.

Romance blossomed and on 24th April 1887, William married Louisa at St Andrew's Church, Nuthurst. The marriage was witnessed by William's friend and brother-in-law, Edwin Leppard and his wife, Alice. Edwin's family were well known throughout Mannings Heath as farmers, blacksmiths and publicans. Louisa and William remained teaching at Mannings Heath School, as husband and wife, and living in the School House next door to the school, until Louisa and he retired in May 1913. Louisa died on 18th September of that year from cancer of the uterus.

---

59 Exeter & Plymouth Gazette.

Chapter 10: 1870 – The Wesleyan/Methodist Elementary School 65

The Mannings Heath School House on Golding Lane. The school was located immediately to the right of the School House.

After Louisa's death, William went to live with his brother, Walter, at Hillbrow (the house known today as "Igls") opposite the Dun Horse. The room on the Horsham end of the house and adjacent to the Brighton Road was his and, from there, he could keep watch over village comings and goings.

William was clearly much loved and respected by many. There are a number of reports in the West Sussex County Times of letters he received from his former school pupils serving at the front in the 1914-1918 Great War. In May 1914, Ernest Cowdry, then a Corporal, wrote to William about a "near miss" from a German shell that hit the adjacent cavalry stables. Ernest had been a pupil at Mannings Heath School from 1894 to 1903. He left the school at age 13, having passed his Labour Certificate qualifications. He wrote again in January 1916, telling William all about the heavy shelling over the Christmas period. He signed himself "One of the Old School Boys".

In May 1918, William received a post card from one of the Worcester brothers (probably Sidney or Ernest, who were both taught by William for eight years, and Sydney reached Standard 5, which is just one below the highest level).

He was, by then, a Lance Corporal and working for the Germans as a prisoner of war and a gardener. In that same month, Ernest Cowdry wrote to him again describing the battle which had resulted in the award of the Military Medal to him. He signed off with the words "from one of your old school boys".

William died in 1937, at "Hillbrow", at the ripe old age of 84, having made a huge contribution to the teaching of many Heathens and to the life of the whole village.

Chapter 11

The Small, Private School

Chapter 13 deals with more of the "wheeling and dealing" events leading up to the building of the new school but, before we get there, we need to say a little about two other small schools that were extant in the village at that time.

The first of these was a private school near the Dun Horse pub.

The Leppard family had been well established in Nuthurst and Mannings Heath from before 1820; the Sussex Election of 1820 Role of Electors for the first Parliament in the reign of George IV has John Leppard listed as entitled to vote as the owner of land and property in the Parish of Nuthurst. The 1841 Census has the family established as farmers and blacksmiths in Mannings Heath. It is difficult to be sure from the records but the indications are that the family owned one or more houses, and land in the vicinity of the Dun Horse pub. John, as a blacksmith, owned the forge opposite the Dun Horse shown on the 1841 Tythe Map in Chapter 3.

In 1871, the family, headed by 61-year-old John, lived at Rose Villa in Mannings Heath. The family consisted of John and his wife, Jane, and their son, Henry. Their daughter, Mary Ann had married a man named Cooper, but was widowed in her 30s. Mary Anne Cooper and her three children Annie, Frederick and Fanny were part of the Rose Villa household of three generations. Rose Villa, as a house name, no longer exists and has not existed since before 1939.

It is Fanny who is of most interest to us in the "teaching" context. The 1881 census has Fanny identified as a "scholar" aged 16. This is most unusual as a daughter would normally be engaged in work after the age of 12, so it suggests that Fanny was bright and still being educated at 16.

The first indication of there being a further school in Mannings Heath comes in Augusta's diaries. On 14th September 1882, she writes, "…Saw F. Cooper's nice little party of seven, they seem improving". On 1st November 1882, Augusta writes, "… Looked in at Fanny's little school, as did Rev McCarogher. Wish I could help them more definitely".

So, Augusta's first hint at Fanny Cooper running a school is in 1882, when she was just 17 years old. This suggests that the 1881 census reference to Fanny being a "scholar" is perhaps more correctly interpreted as Fanny being a young teacher.

We do not know where the school was housed. It might have been in the family home, Rose Villa, but perhaps there is an interesting alternative. There have been persistent rumours of there being a school known as the Dun Horse school. One possibility is that was a "nick name" for the Methodist School because William Reading lived at the Dun Horse and his parents were the publicans. However, another possibility is that Fanny ran her "little" school in a room in the Dun Horse and it was, in fact, her school that was known as the Dun Horse school. One of those little "local history" puzzles that may never be conclusively resolved!

The next reference to Fanny's school is to be found in ref. 65 – the Parish Magazines. The magazine for May 1886 records, "Some hope is being entertained of uniting Miss Cooper's little school *(which had, by then, been operating for about five years)* with one under Government at Mannings Heath, but nothing can be arranged until the proposition has been considered by the Committee". This is, presumably, a reference to the school Management Committee chaired by Rev. McCarogher.

The unification did occur with the best of results for Fanny. On 26th July 1886, she was taken on as Assistant Mistress at Mannings Heath school and her eight (at the time) pupils also transferred to the school.

Those pupils are identified, from the Register (ref. 1) as coming from a "Private School" and they are: -

Edward Henley
Frederic and Elizabeth Fuller
Ellen Barnard
Ethel, Frederic and Harry Leppard
Edward Wells

Fanny is shown in the 1911 census as an Elementary School Teacher, so was presumably still teaching at Mannings Heath school. Her death was registered in Brighton in 1916 when she was just 51 years old.

Chapter 12

The Forest School, Coolhurst

I am indebted to Mark Scrase Dickins of Coolhurst Manor for the loan of a fascinating, sixty-five page document written by Frederick Fuller: "Memories of the 1860s" being his record of life in Mannings Heath, Nuthurst and Coolhurst in that period[60].

Frederick was born in 1850 in Mannings Heath, on the border with Coolhurst, at Fullers Farm, now part of the Mannings Heath Golf Club property in Goldings Lane. He was the youngest of five children born to Henry and Kezia Fuller.

A drawing of the Fullers Farm house in Frederick's
"Memories", probably drawn by him from childhood memory.

His parents both died when he was about 10 years old and his upbringing came under the authority of the Aldridge family of St Leonards House. When he was 11 years old, he is recorded as lodging with the Askey family in Colgate.

---

60 Memories of the 1860s by Frederick Fuller.

He was a gardener all his working life and, in 1881, he married Helen Gresty in Chorlton, Lancashire. When he was 51, he and his family emigrated to New Zealand, which is where he wrote his "Memories", whilst in lodgings in Auckland. He died in 1932, aged 82 and is buried in the Waikumte Cemetary, Auckland.

The grave of Frederick Fuller, and his son,
John, in Waikumete Cemetery, New Zealand.

Frederick received his education initially at the Nuthurst Sunday School and the Nuthurst Day School (presumably what is now St Andrew's School and one of the schools mentioned in the 1833 survey – see Chapter 3). Charles Jupp was the school master and Augusta Bigg made frequent visits and did some teaching.

Having misbehaved himself in the Nuthurst Sunday School, Frederick was taken away and sent to the Forest Church Sunday School which was run by Lady Elizabeth Dickins. From his description of events, this probably happened when Frederick was 9 years old, so in 1859.

Chapter 12: The Forest School, Coolhurst

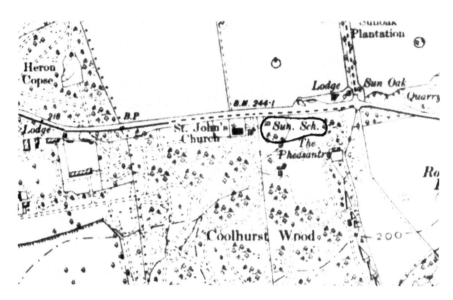

This extract from the 1874 Ordnance Survey map of Coolhurst shows the Sunday School next to St John's Church.

The map identifies the school as a "Sunday School" but, in fact, the Scrase Dickins family had built a day school in that location probably in about 1860. From the Scrase Dickins records, we have a sketch of the church that shows a building in the background that looks as though it might have been a small school building.

Sketch of St John's Church, Coolhurst, and a possible school building in the background. The sketch shows the church before the 1889 major extensions and changes to the building structure.

The first teacher was a Miss Groombridge but she was soon replaced by Elizabeth Venus who was the daughter of George Venus, farm bailiff to the Scrase Dickins at Coolhurst and living at the Coolhurst Farm House.

Frederick describes Elizabeth Venus as having "… no special training or aptitude for teaching, consequently the school was conducted in a happy-go-lucky style." The school worked on the monitorial system with the older, more able teaching the younger and less able. Frederick taught the boys class so we are probably looking at a date of around 1863, when Frederick would have been 13.

We know that the Forest School was still functioning in 1883 because ref. 1 shows children joining the new Mannings Heath School from Forest School in September 1883. Those children were Emily Holder, aged 10, Sarah Holder, aged 6, Muriel Boniface, aged 12 and James Highgate, aged 6.

It seems likely that the opening of the Mannings Heath School served to provide an alternative and led to the closure of the Forest School sometime between 1883 and 1904; the 1904 Ordnance Survey map makes no reference to any school close to St John's Church.

We will see, in the next chapter, that the Forest School was used in the arguments and "battles" over the creation of the Mannings Heath School.

Chapter 13

1883 – the Birth of the C.E. School in Mannings Heath

The year of 1883 is central to the birth of the new Mannings Heath School as it is the year in which it opened its doors to its first pupils. But the lead up to this opening started on 15th July 1871. Some of what was happening in this matter in the 1870s is described by Augusta Bigg in her diaries (reference 56).

The tortuous and convoluted progress towards the new Mannings Heath School was started by the LEA with the publication of an Inspector's Report on 15th July 1871 (see ref. 47). This report contained the following key points: -

- The district *(Nuthurst as a whole)* was estimated to contain 675 inhabitants and, as a result, the Inspector calculated that school accommodation was needed for 101 pupils. *(One has to question the need for "estimated" because 1871 was a year in which a National Census was carried out making "estimation" unnecessary.)*
- The existing school will accommodate 76 boys, girls and infants. *(This seems to ignore the Readings in Mannings Heath, the little school run by Fanny Cooper and Forest in Coolhurst, which are all attended by Mannings Heath children.)*
- The report concluded that "An efficient school with accommodation for about 30 children should be provided in Mannings Heath".

Presumably, it was this report that played a part in the events, like the meetings at the Dun Horse, described by Augusta Bigg.

Reference 47 then covers all the formal events leading up to the building of the new Mannings Heath School in 1883.

On 14th June 1872, the LEA issued a revised report concluding that: -

- The population had risen to 699 and therefore, 116 school places were needed.
- The existing school will accommodate 76 and the school in Mannings Heath needs to accommodate 89. *(There is no explanation offered for the arithmetic!)*

Moving on to 1874, the Rev. John McCarogher of Nuthurst enters the debate in a letter to the LEA of 21st January 1874, saying that: -

- The Methodist School (Readings) in Mannings Heath is a private school and not under his control.
- St Andrew's School in Nuthurst has been enlarged to admit "likely additional children".

(The letter clearly suggests that he is not in favour of a new school in Mannings Heath but that the Nuthurst School (St Andrew's) will meet the needs of the entire parish.)

The LEA's response was quick – a letter on 24th January 1874 – and bluntly to the point: -

- The Nuthurst School, although enlarged, does not provide an "efficient" education solution for Mannings Heath.
- The existing private school *(Readings)* should be closed so that the "new school" is "efficient".

(There is no description by the LEA of what they mean by "efficient", but it is a word often used by them as a reason for their decisions.)

The debate continues throughout 1874 with Rev. McCarogher continuing to argue against a new school for Mannings Heath. In a letter to the LEA of 1st July 1874, he argues: -

- The enlarged school of St Andrew's, Nuthurst, is the answer and is working well.
- He refers to the "small school at Coolhurst", although not by its name of Forest, as being able to provide part of the "efficient" solution for Mannings Heath – without the need for building a new school being the implication behind his letter.

At last, the LEA is recorded as actually visiting Nuthurst (on 29th May 1875) to look at the situation "on the ground" – and one can be sure that "about time too" would have been a common sentiment. They pointed out to Rev McCarogher that his reference to the school at Coolhurst could not form part of providing a proper solution for schooling in Mannings Heath.

On 14th October 1882, Amos made the case again and enclosed a plan and elevation drawing of Readings. In Chapter 8 – all about Amos Chart – I

Chapter 13: 1883 – the Birth of the C.E. School in Mannings Heath

mentioned his first move in the fray and his letter to the LEA of 28th June. This letter was also signed by Robert Reading (William Reading's father), Robert Lewry and two others. Amos formally requested the LEA to carry out an "examination of the children (54 scholars including 20 infants) attending". This was clearly aimed at making the case for Readings to become the school for Mannings Heath.

This provoked a response and the LEA came and inspected Readings. Their report on 24th October 1882, was not favourable. It pointed out a number of perceived deficiencies in the structure and layout of Readings, including no playground, poor toilets and single brick walls in places.

But Amos was not done yet.

On 8th November 1882, he wrote again to the LEA rebutting their general concerns about the toilets, lack of playground and generally poor building construction by writing that "… so healthy is the site that there have been no occasions to close the school for any sickness since its opening nearly thirteen years ago".

So, towards the end of 1882, after ten years of wheeling, dealing and wrangling, the situation with regards to a "proper" and "efficient" school in Mannings Heath had come down to: -

- The Church of England, through Rev. McCarogher, proposing that a combination of increased capacity at St Andrew's School in Nuthurst, plus use of the Forest School in Coolhurst would meet the needs of Mannings Heath.
- The Methodists, through Amos Chart, proposing that the existing Methodist – Readings – School should become the "official" Mannings Heath School.
- The LEA, in effect, saying "a plague on both your houses" and advocating the closure of Readings and building a new, purpose-built school in Mannings Heath.

In December 1882, Amos made proposals to the LEA, presumably along the lines of what he proposed to Rev McCarogher in January. Amos was probably not aware that an Education Department internal meeting had reviewed this proposal and concluded that development of the Methodist school *(Readings)* was not the right solution and that the proposal could not be supported.

It was in January 1883, that Amos made his final attempt to win the battle to have Readings recognised as the Mannings Heath School – and it was a bold move that he made, described by Augusta in her diary entry for 20th January 1883.

Amos had written to Rev McCarogher, and possibly others, asking if the Mannings Heath ratepayers "...would give £100 towards enlarging their *(the Methodist's)* school, which doesn't satisfy the examiners *(This is a reference to the Inspector's report of October 1882)*, and £10 a year towards current expenses".

It is not difficult to anticipate Rev McCarogher's response, shared by Augusta, that "...handing our children over to secularists & dissenters, which seems to me very wrong in principle." This comment seems strangely at odds with the de facto situation and Augusta's support for Readings, and the teaching, by William, of at least fifty of the Mannings Heath children in the "dissenters" existing school, which she apparently admired.

However, this final effort by Amos did make a big impact in provoking a "meeting of ratepayers" on 2nd February 1883. This meeting was fully reported in the Sussex Agricultural Express of 6th February and is worth recording, in full.

"THE NEW SCHOOL AT MANNINGS HEATH. - On Friday evening a meeting of ratepayers was held to consider what steps should be taken with regard to the new school ordered by Government to be erected at Mannings Heath. For upwards of 12 years a school has been carried on at that place in a building formerly used as a Wesleyan Chapel. After a recent inspection the inspector reported 'The children that attend there are suitably taught, and pass on the whole a very fair examination; I wish the premises were efficient.' The Education Department thereupon issued an order for a new school. The managers of the present one have sent a circular to each ratepayer, pointing out the expense a School Board would entail and offering to rebuild their school according to Government requirements, and maintain it as a Public Elementary School, provided the inhabitants of the parish would furnish £100 towards the rebuilding, and £10 per annum towards the teacher's salary. This offer was rejected; as was also a very liberal one from C.S.S. Dickins, Esq., of Newells, to build a school if the ratepayers would agree to pay interest on the money it would cost, which would be given back as a yearly subscription towards its support. The third proposition, 'That a school be built by public subscription,' was carried, and a committee, consisting of Messrs. R. Henderson, S.H. Bigg, H. Leppard, G.H. Gander, and Muggeridge, was appointed to carry the decision into effect. Subscriptions amounting to £390 were announced. Sir W.W. Burrell, Bart M.P. promising £50; Mr., Mrs., and Miss Bigg, £50; Mr. R. Henderson, £50; Colonel

Chapter 13: 1883 – the Birth of the C.E. School in Mannings Heath

Aldridge, £20 and Mr Dickins, £20."

If it did nothing else, the inspection report confirmed the excellent work being done by William Reading under conditions that were far from ideal.

So, in the end, this final effort by Amos had a real healing effect within the community because it brought the Established Church and the Methodists together, behind the new school, and ensured that the school would be a Church school, with religious education embedded in the curriculum, and not a secular Board school, which the 1870 act would have allowed.

Having reached this point, things began to move quickly. On 16th February, Augusta records attending a school meeting, held at Swallowfield, where she notes that: -

- Mr Dickens *(She means Charles Scrace Dickins of Coolhurst)* will sell us a bit of ground.
- Six builders are invited to send in tenders.

The conveyance for the ground[61] makes no reference to price and the land was not sold but gifted, under various Acts of Parliament, covering gifting sites for school building and, in particular, "for the education of the Poor". The land was conveyed to be in the charge of the Rector and Church Wardens of Nuthurst and their successors and included the land for the erection of a "residence for the School Master or School Mistress". The conveyance also stipulated that the school was "...to be under the Management of the Rector and Church Wardens... professing the principles of the Established Church". In effect, this conveyance set the terms of management of the school, giving both the Diocese and the LEA or Education Board, the rights to inspect operation of the school and its educational performance and to agree the curriculum. This solved one of the concerns expressed by Rev McCarogher, that the new school would be purely secular with no Church of England or biblical teaching.

For John McCarogher, this was not just a concern but very much a matter of deep faith and belief. This became very obvious in April 1891, at a celebration of John McCarogher's forty years as Rector of Nuthurst. The celebration was reported in the Sussex Agricultural Express of 21st April 1891. In his closing words, John McCarogher is reported as saying that, "It had been his desire to

---

61 Conveyance of the land for the Mannings Heath School.

provide schools where the poor people of the parish could be brought up in the principles of the Church of England, and as long as he had breath in his body, he would ward off the abomination of a Board school in the parish. To leave out religion from instruction given in the schools was to bring a child down to the level of a beast".

By 26th February, the builder's quotes were in and the builder, Dewdney, selected with a quote of £285. By July, there was substantial building progress and Augusta was able to write "Went to new school, all nice" and, by Monday 9th September, the new school was able to open.

Augusta records that there was a gathering of twenty-three children at an evening meeting in the (what Augusta calls) "Church Room" on Sunday 9th September. This is her Mission Church, now known as the Church of the Good Shepherd. The purpose of the gathering was for the first teacher at the new school – Mrs Annie Farrer – to make the acquaintance of the children before the first official day of term on Monday 10th September.

She goes on to record that only fourteen of the twenty-three are going to be starting at the new school. She writes, "I would not take any means to get them away from Reading who has got most of them, I think, to promise him. We must feel our way and make it a work of faith and prayer but the mere fact of having an earnest, good woman living here must be a helpful influence."

Author's Note: -
Augusta is clearly concerned. William Reading has done what he can to try and secure continuity of his teaching career by "persuading" pupils to stay with him. This is significant because Readings School has some fifty pupils who should make up the bulk of the C.E./Board School intake. Without that intake, the whole viability of the new school would be jeopardised.

On Monday 10th September 1883, Augusta records that "The clergy *(her emphasis!)* opened new school". Both Augustas – mother and daughter – took afternoon tea at the school and Augusta (daughter) comments that "Mrs F. making a beginning and seeming very painstaking…" There were just three families of children present – the Bonifaces (5) from St Andrew's in Nuthurst, the Highgates (5) from Readings and the Holders (4) from Forest. Augusta put up several pictures and said a few words of prayer, begging that there might be no quarrelling with Readings school. *(Augusta was clearly very concerned about the difficult situation and no doubt torn between her admiration for what William Reading had achieved and concern for the future of the new school).*

Chapter 13: 1883 – the Birth of the C.E. School in Mannings Heath

Augusta continues writing, "The general feeling seems to be that it would be unfair to take the children from Reading, who set up a useful school when there was none, and has taught well, and, as few know or care much about religious teaching, one rather respects the feeling. But can Government compel us to keep a school for 15 children?"

The school Register (contained with ref. 1) shows that the initial intake of fourteen children grew gradually through the first term to a total of twenty-one, with pupils coming from Christ Church, Worthing, St Andrew's in Nuthurst, from Colgate and three more from Readings.

It was on Monday 21st January 1884, Augusta records, with obvious relief and delight, that the "...fusion of the two Mannings Heath schools took place". William Reading was asked to be taken on as assistant master, under Annie Farrer as Head. After a meeting, this was accepted. Rev McCarogher carried out the opening and Augusta records it as a "Perfect day".

Author's Note: For Miss Augusta, the daughter, this whole series of events had been a real "roller coaster" ride testing emotions, Christian beliefs and concerns for the young of Mannings Heath. The diaries provide a remarkable insight into her feelings and a background to the prosaic business actions and "wheeling and dealing" throughout the 1870s and early 80s – all to do with setting up an elementary school for about seventy pupils. The diaries outline that there are times when the human race is its own worst enemy but, that with patience and steadfastness, the right result can be achieved.

This story has introduced us to four remarkable people – Amos Chart, William Reading, Miss Augusta Bigg and Rev. John McCarogher. Mannings Heath owed them much.

And this is what all the fuss was all about; Mannings Heath School, on Golding Lane, looking towards Coolhurst, in about 1900, with the old Drill Hall behind it (the Drill Hall has been replaced by the Community Centre). The Common lies opposite the school on the other side of Golding Lane and the School House is to the left of the school, behind the boy wearing the boater. The gentleman on the right of the picture looks like William Reading.

There is no architect plan drawing of the school so this plan has been constructed from scaling photographs and from a simple valuation survey sketch in the National Archive records.

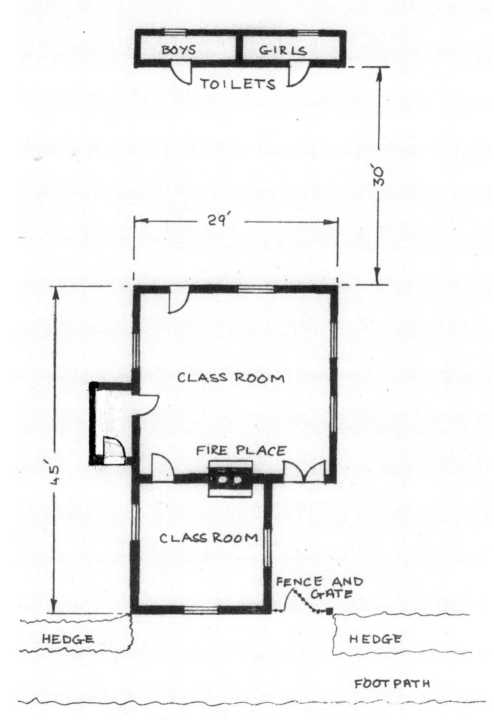

Chapter 14

1883/4 – The First Academic Year

On 10th September 1883, there was a gathering of new pupils for the new school to meet the Head Teacher and also the Augustas – mother and daughter. In her diary, Augusta (daughter) writes that "Mrs F. making a beginning and seeming very painstaking". The "Mrs F." was the new Head Teacher, Annie Marian Farrer. Annie was born in 1845 in Bognor Regis, so was 38 years of age when she became Head Teacher. (See Appendix 3)

Perhaps the best way to appreciate how the new school took shape is to draw on Annie's own words in the Head Teacher's Log Book for that first year (see ref. 1): the following is a transcript of what she wrote.

September 10th. Annie Marian Farrer (Mistress 2nd Class) opened this (Mannings Heath) School on this date with 13 children. The Rector *(Rev John McCarogher)* read prayers. Mrs and Miss Bigg visited during the afternoon. *(Augusta records this visit in her diary and comments "All so new and clean and children good. Mrs F. making a beginning and seeming very painstaking, especially noticing the sing-song reading").*

September 11th. Col. Aldridge and family visited this afternoon. Mistress examined school children and placed them in their respective standards. Thus Standard 5, 1 boy, Standard 3, 2 boys, Standard 2, 1 boy and 2 girls, Standard 1, 1 boy and 1 girl, Infants 5. *(The Aldridge family of St Leonards House and the Scrace Dickins family, of Coolhurst, who gifted the land for the school, are related by marriage and both families owned significant areas of Mannings Heath land.)*

September 17th. Admitted 5 new children from Monk's Gate. Miss Bigg visited. The Rector called in the morning and the Rev. Spalding (Curate) in the afternoon.

September 19th. Mrs and Miss Bigg visited, also Lady "Tite". *(Annie is clearly unsure who this visitor was. It was, in fact, Lady Tite who was Mrs Augusta Bigg's sister.)*

Chapter 14: 1883/4 – The First Academic Year

September 27th. Mr Scrase called concerning the Highgates. *(Mr Scrase is the Board's Attendance Officer responsible for the school. No known connection with the Scrace Dickins family, just a coincidence.)*

October 5th. The Rector and Miss McCarogher visited school this morning. Admitted 2 new children from Tattleson's Farm today. *(Tattleson's Farm is in Colgate).* Received some new books this week for all classes.

October 12th. The Rector visited this week. Mrs Bigg also visited.

October 19th. Rev J. McCarogher and Mrs McCarogher visited. Admitted 3 new children from Readings School. Taught the children a new song.

October 26th. Mrs and Miss McCarogher visited during the week, also Mrs Bigg and Miss Curtis.

November 2nd. Rev McCarogher visited school this week, also Rev Spalding.

November 9th. Work as usual. Miss Bigg visited.

November 16th. Mrs McCarogher visited school.

November 23rd. Miss Bigg visited and took 1st and 2nd classes for Reading. Mistress taught the children a new song. A new clock for school. *(1st and 2nd classes probably means the children at Standards 1 and 2.)*

November 30th. Received some needlework for the girls from Mrs Bigg who visited and took Standard 1 for Reading.

December 7th. Work as usual. Ettie Holder being ill is sent this week to the Children's Convalescent Home, Brighton, for 3 weeks by Miss Bigg.

December 14th. Mr Scrase, Attendance Officer, called concerning the payments of school fees for Highgates. Mother to apply to the Board for necessary money.

December 17th. Examined Registers and I found them correct. J.O. McCarogher.

December 21st. Closed School this week for Christmas Holiday. To re-open January 1st 1884.

January 1st, 1884. School re-opened this week, no new children. Rev J.O. McCarogher visited on Wednesday. Children had their treat on the Saturday.

January 10th. Mistress attended a Committee Meeting concerning the school on this date. *(This would have been a School Managers Committee Meeting chaired by Rev McCarogher.)* Mr Scrase (Attendance Officer) called concerning the Highgates money – paid in 1s 4d for 4 weeks of last quarter from the Guardians. Four children to be paid for, for the future.

January 16th. Miss McCarogher visited school this morning concerning the books etc. required from the National Society.

January 18th. Work as usual. Mrs Bigg and Miss Curtis visited during the week.

January 21st. Admitted 52 children from Mr Reading's school. Rev J.O. McCarogher visited school and read prayers. Miss McCarogher visited, sent for books etc. from the National Society. Mr William Reading, having been appointed Assistant Master by the committee of the school, entered upon his duties. *(It is this which Augusta describes as a "Perfect day". The meeting on January 10th, attended by Annie, was, presumably, to discuss the matter of the amalgamation of the two schools and the appointment, to the new school, of William Reading.)*

January 22nd. Mrs Bigg and Miss Curtis visited. Received a supply of needlework from Mrs McCarogher.

January 29th. Received a supply of new books for all classes, pictures for Infants all from National Society. Sent for two new Time Tables as the work of the one now in use is hardly suitable for the number of children we now have. Rev McCarogher visited during the week, also Mrs Bigg.

February 8th. Mrs McCarogher visited this week and Miss Bigg came at 9.15 and remained in the school until 12 o'clock. Admitted 1 new child. Entered Object Lessons for infants on Page 5. *("Page 5" refers to the page number in the Log Book and included Objects for Infants and Standard 1 pupils and Poems for Standards 1 to 5. All as reproduced below.)*

Page 5.
List of Object Lessons – Infants and Standard 1.
Animals

- The Sheep
- The Cow
- The Cat
- The Dog

- The Horse
- The Goat

Minerals

- Coal
- Slate
- Butter
- Trees
- Water
- Wind

Poetry

- Standard 1 – The Robin (Hardy)
- Standard 2 – Birds Nests (John Clare)
- Standard 3 – We are Seven (Wordsworth)
- Standard 4 – Lucy Grey (Wordsworth)
- Standard 5 – The Spanish Armada (Macaulay) and The Burial of Sir John Moore (Wolfe)

Author's Note: -
The basis for "Object Lessons" is best described by N.A. Calkins[62]. Calkins writes that "Observation is the absolute basis for all knowledge. The first object in education must be to lead a child to observe with accuracy; the second, to express with correctness the results of the observations." This basis, taken from Calkin's book, shows clearly why Object Lessons were a major feature of Elementary Education.

February 12th. Miss Bigg visited at 10am and remained until 12 o'clock. *(Augusta, in her diary, tells us that she taught singing and reading and that "All seems to work well". She then taught rounds to the best singers.)*

February 15th. Miss Bigg visited and remained all the morning, taking a class for reading and singing. Mistress taught the children a new song "'Hurrah' for England".

(Augusta writes in her diary that she spent three hours at the school and there was an "interesting" Bible reading on The Flood with the older ones, then rounds, then reading, all seeming to go well. She gave the school a skipping rope for play time and a trap, bat and ball.)

---

62 Primary Object Lessons, N.A. Calkins.

Author's Note: -
This description of the events of February 22nd is taken from Augusta's diary and is not mentioned in the Log Book. Augusta called on Mrs Wickens. As we saw earlier, the Wickens were ardent Methodists and must have been very concerned about the events described in Chapter 13 and, in particular, about the loss of "their Methodist school". Augusta writes "Talked about Church and dissent; she thanked me so and said she was so glad we were not so divided as she thought. She sometimes yearned for the services of the Church in which she was brought up and confirmed (presumably this refers to the Church of England) but they did not dare leave for fear of chastisement. Students delighted with new school and liked my Bible class and Mrs F and her's..."

This conversation must have brought much relief to Augusta and confirmed that the "machinations" described in Chapter 13 had not created long term, deep divisions within the Mannings Heath community.

In her diary entry for February 25th, Augusta writes "...Mrs Farrer and Reading work well together and everyone seems pleased with the fusion of the two schools! May all this make us truly thankful and help us trust in future".

March 1st. Divided the 4th Class into 2 sections, as many of the children are very backward. A good attendance this week. Rev Spalding *(the Curate)* visited and closed school with a prayer.

March 8th. Miss McCarogher and Rev J.O. McCarogher visited during the week also Miss Bigg who came at 9.15 and remained until 11 o'clock. Taught the Infants and 1st Standard a new story. Rev Spalding visited school and read prayers in the afternoon. *Augusta writes "3 hours at new school – all seems to go well..."*

March 10th. Miss McCarogher visited school and brought Government Papers to say the examinations to be held in May. School year ends April 30th. *For Mannings Heath and the new school, this was a momentous event. It would be the first time that pupil standards and achievement would be measured on an Education Authority basis. Readings, as a private school, had never been subjected to such testing.*

March 11th. Miss Bigg visited school at 9.15 and remained until 12 o'clock.

March 12th. Miss Aldridge and Lady... visited school in the afternoon, heard children sing. Mrs Bigg came in the morning at 10 and remained until 12 o'clock.

Chapter 14: 1883/4 – The First Academic Year

March 19th. Rev McCarogher visited school during the morning and ordered more hooks to be placed in the porch for the boy's caps. Began knitting with the boys (infants).

March 28th. Received Government papers for the examinations.

March 31st. Miss Bigg visited and remained all the morning.

April 1st. Miss Bigg visited and brought knitting cotton.

April 4th. Rev Spalding visited during the week. Mistress taught Infants a new song "Hop, hop, hop".

April 10th. No school on April 11th as it is Good Friday.

Augusta writes that "New school works well. I go up once or twice a week to give Bible lessons, teach singing and hear reading". Augusta seems well content with progress in what, to her, is almost a personal endeavour and she is clearly making a big personal contribution towards its success. There is no hint in the Head Teacher's Log Book that the input, from Augusta, is anything but welcomed.

April 14th. Opened school on Easter Monday. Miss Bigg sent flower seeds for the children.

April 28th. Entry by the Rector. "Visited the school. Checked the register. Satisfied with the behaviour and order of the children. J.O. McCarogher."

May 1st. Received from Rev McCarogher the notice of date (May 16th) for H.M. Inspector's visit at 10 in the morning. *(This was another milestone – the first formal Authority inspection of Mannings Heath School.)*

May 7th. Mrs and Miss Bigg visited during the week. Also Rev Spalding.

May 12th. Rev J.O. McCarogher visited school. Checked the register and stayed ¾ of an hour.

May 16th. Examination Day. *(The Log Book records the attendance of George French as the Inspector.)*

The Log Book contains notes by the Head Teacher for upcoming events. The first is the songs she prepares the children to sing as part of the Examination.

The songs are: -

Seniors.

1. When cooling morning breezes
2. Hurrah for England
3. How doth the little busy bee
4. We shall meet but we shall miss him
5. Give me a draught from the crystal spring
6. The Blue Bells of Scotland
7. I hear thunder (sung as a round)

Infants.

1. Mary had a little lamb
2. The neat little clock (sung with actions)
3. Hot cross buns
4. Tread (sung with actions)

The second set of notes is preparing for the next school year (1885).

Poetry for: -
Standard 1. Good night, good morning.
Standard 2. Wandering Willie.
Standard 3. The Inchcape Rock. (Southey)
Standard 4. The wreck of the Hesperus. (Longfellow)
Standard 5. The May Queen. (Tennyson)

Object Lessons for Infants: -

1. A watch
2. Sponge
3. The rabbit
4. A birds nest
5. Sugar
6. Chalk
7. Flock of animals
8. Fishes
9. Colours
10. An apple
11. Salt
12. The eye

Chapter 14: 1883/4 – The First Academic Year

May 22nd. Received the "Duplicate" from H.M. Inspector. Rev McCarogher visited. *(There is no explanation of "Duplicate" but it could well be a duplicate of the Inspector's report following the inspection and examinations carried out on 16th May. A hand written copy of the report is in the Log Book following the 14th July entry.)*

May 26th. Admitted 2 new children. Several of the elder ones have left. *(The two children joining were both 4 years old and this was their first school. The leavers were from one family in Monks Gate suggesting that there was a family reason for their leaving.)*

June 1st. School closed for Whitsuntide holiday. One week.

June 9th. School re-opened. Admitted 3 fresh children. Miss Bigg visited.

June 16th. Admitted 2 new children.

June 23rd. Admitted 1 fresh child.

June 30th. Work as usual. Miss Bigg visited.

July 7th. Miss Bigg kindly brought some blinds for the window. Rev McCarogher visited. Received notice of the Diocesan Inspection.

July 11th. Rev R. Blight visited and examined the children in Scripture. *(Although not stated, this was, in fact, the Diocesan Inspection.)* Mrs Bigg gave the children notice of her intention to give them a treat on the 29th.

Jul 14th. Rev McCarogher visited.

Copy of H.M. Inspector's Report. *(Following the inspection carried out on 16th May.)*

Nuthurst, Mannings Heath C.E. School.

The Managers have provided a very nice, pleasant little school here. The number of children in attendance shows plainly how greatly it was needed. The results of the Examination in Elementary Subjects are creditable on the whole. The reading needs particular care. The English was not sufficiently advanced for the Grant to be recommended. The sewing is well taught. Mrs Farrer deserves praise for what she has done.

Infants Class: The class rooms not very large and its ventilation should be improved. The infants need a great deal of care and attention to bring them to a satisfactory state as to Elementary attainments.

J.O. McCarogher   **Annie Marian Farrer C.M. 2nd Class**

July 11th and July 14th – Log Book Entries made by Rev J.O. McCarogher.

The Rev Robert Blight, Diocesan Inspector of Schools examined the children in the different Standards and expressed his satisfaction with their answers. Signed the Merit Cards awarded by the Diocesan Inspector. Registers and found them correct. Found the school in excellent order.

J.O. McCarogher

July 18th. Work as usual this week.

July 22nd. **Copy of the Diocesan Inspector's Report.**

Report of Religious Instruction in the Nuthurst, Mannings Heath School.
Inspected July 11th 1884

Old Testament – Good
New Testament – Good
Catechism – Good
Repetition – Good

General Remarks. It is not too much to say that this school is a great boon to the district in which it stands. The necessity for it may be gathered from the fact that there are already nearly 80 children in it.

Mrs Farrer is a careful teacher and has begun her work well. The knowledge hitherto imparted is elementary, but thoroughly practical and good, and the foundation of future excellence is being carefully laid. Mr Reading deserves praise for his work with the younger children.

I would offer my earnest congratulations to the Manager on the success that has attended his efforts to provide a school in this part of the Parish.

Signed: **Robert Blight – Diocesan Inspector**   **J.O. McCarogher**

July 29th. Children had their Summer Treat at Swallowfield Park which was kindly given by Mrs and Miss Bigg. Rev McCarogher visited school during the

Chapter 14: 1883/4 – The First Academic Year

week. Children to break up for their Summer Vacation for one month. To re-assemble September 1st.

This was the last Log Book entry for the first year of Mannings Heath School. It was a momentous year, full of "firsts", and it reflected well on the work of Annie Farrer and on William Reading, and also on the support to the new school from the Rector, Rev McCarogher, and the Biggs – mother and daughter.

Chapter 15

Reflections on the First Year of the Mannings Heath School

Appendix 2 contains details (from ref. 50) of pupils admitted to the school in the first year – from September 1883 to July 1884. In summary there were: -

- A total of 94 admissions.
- 23 of the admissions left in the year, leaving an average of 80 pupils present in the year.
- Of the 80, 32 were infants aged from 3 to 7 and 48 were pupils aged from 8 to the oldest at 14.

As an observation, the effective "management" of the start-up of a brand-new school and coping with this range of ages and the numbers in the pupil intake speaks volumes for the abilities of Annie Farrer, as Head, and William Reading, as Assistant. The fact that the two formal school inspections in the year, as contained in Chapter 11, resulted in very positive reports is to their huge credit.

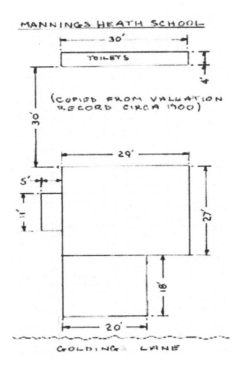

Plan of Mannings Heath School from the valuation survey[63].

---

63 Plan of Mannings Heath School from National Archives records. ED21/17544.

Chapter 15: Reflections on the First Year of the Mannings Heath School

We do not know for sure but it seems likely that the older pupils would have used the larger room as their class room and the infants would have used the smaller room facing on to Golding Lane.

If this is correct then the older pupils would have had a personal space of about $3^1/_2$ x 4 ft per pupil and the infants about 3x3 ft per pupil. This is a big improvement on the space in Readiings for older and infant children, but the more limited space for the infants does explain the criticism made by the H.M. Inspector in his report of 16th May 1884, with regard to space and ventilation in the infant's classroom. Nevertheless, a big improvement in facilities. So, what was the teaching like in one of the new schools built in response to the 1870 Foster Act? We are fortunate, in West Sussex, to have a book entitled "Scholars and Slates – Sussex Schools in the 1880s" (see ref. 51).

Ref. 51 includes a document entitled "Standards of Examination", from which extracts are included below. And this is what would have been taught to the "Heathens" and what they would have been examined against.

Standard	Reading	Writing	Arithmetic	Grammar, Geography & History
1	To read a short paragraph from a book not confined to words of one syllable.	Copy in manuscript character a line of print on slate or in copy book and write from dictation a few common words.	Notation and numeration up to 1,000. Simple addition and subtraction of numbers of not more than four figures. Multiplication up to 6 times 12.	
2	To read with intelligence a short paragraph from an elementary reading book.	A sentence from the same book, slowly read once, then dictated. Copy of large or half text.	Notation and numeration up to 100,000. The four simple rules of short division.	Point out nouns in passages written or read. Define points of compass, motions of the earth, the meaning of a map.
3	To read with intelligence a short paragraph from a more advanced reading book.	A sentence slowly dictated once from the same book. Copy books to be shown (small hand, capital letters and figures).	Notation and numeration up to 1,000,000. Long division and compound addition and subtraction (money).	Point out the nouns, verbs and adjectives. Outlines of geography of England with special knowledge of the school's county.

Standard	Reading	Writing	Arithmetic	Grammar, Geography & History
4	To read with intelligence a few lines of prose or poetry selected by the Inspector.	Eight lines slowly dictated once from a reading book. Copy books to be shown (improved small hand).	Compound rules (money) and reduction (common weights and measures).	Parsing of a simple sentence. Outlines of Geography of Great Britain, Ireland and Colonies. Outlines of History of England to Norman Conquest.
5	Improved reading.	Writing from memory the substance of a short story read out twice; spelling, grammar and handwriting to be considered.	Practice, bills of parcels and simple proportion.	Parsing with analysis of a simple sentence. Outlines of geography of Europe – physical and political. Outlines of History of England from Norman Conquest to accession of Henry VII.
6	Reading with fluency and expression.	A short theme or letter, the composition, spelling, grammar and handwriting to be considered.	Proportion, vulgar and decimal fractions.	Parsing and analysis – complex sentence. Outline of World geography. History of England; Henry VII – George III

Notes to Standards

In History and Geography, pupils should show special knowledge of events and features with a local connection.

Reading is to show intelligence and not just memory.

In Arithmetic, the work of girls is to be judged more leniently than of boys.

Weights and measures studied should be those of use in the context of industrial occupations of the district.

Chapter 15: Reflections on the First Year of the Mannings Heath School

(These notes are an interpretation of the ref. 51 original).

So, what was to be taught was well prescribed, focussed on what was useful and progress was examined every year. One could observe that the Victorians knew what mattered to meet the needs of the nation, in a situation where industrial leaders were concerned about the need to improve education to be able to more effectively compete with our European rivals. *(Some things never change – where have we heard this subsequently?!)*

The report by the Inspector for the inspection carried out in May states that "The English was not sufficiently advanced for the Grant to be recommended". This is hardly surprising as the school had been running for only a few months before this inspection and examination was carried out. However, performance measured and reported upon by the Inspector was the means by which the school received its funding grant, which could mean lower fees paid by the families of the pupils. Grants were calculated by the Inspector on a standard form which took into account attendance, performance and results achieved.

We have seen, in Chapter 14, some of the topics that Annie and William were teaching and were considering for the following year. A typical Sussex school time table is shown below taken from ref. 51.

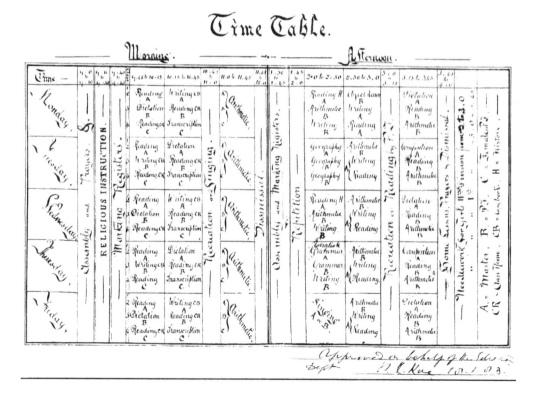

The time table shows very clearly the strong emphasis on the "3 Rs" of Reading, wRiting and aRithmetic. Reading and Arithmetic are shown as single subjects but Writing is included within writing, dictation, composition and transcription.

The timetable shows that about 90% of teaching time was devoted to the "3Rs".

There is a vivid testament to the quality and effectiveness of this teaching in ref. 30 and, specifically, Allen Flint's story in the "Village Voices" section. The correctness of his grammar, his fine use of words, the thoughtful structure of his story, his spelling accuracy, his immaculate handwriting… all bear witness to the effectiveness of his school days. I know this because I typed up Allen's original handwritten manuscript, and Allen completed his formal education at the age of 12 in 1923.

Below are examples, for each of the Standards I to V, of examination arithmetic questions set, and the answers. The questions show very clearly that "number understanding" was expected to be of a high order.

Standard IV

£ 2006)161,357 - 7 -1½ (80 - 8 - 8½ + 1748

Reduce 12 cu. yds. 2 3 cu. ft. 384 cu. in. to cubic inches
Ansr. 600,000 cu. in.

Reduce 900,099 inches to miles
Ansr. 4 m. 1 fur. 25 po. 4½ yds. 2 ft. 3 in.

If one sovereign weighs one hundred and twenty three grains how many can be made out of ten pounds eight dwts. eighteen grains.
Ansr. 470

Standard V

Find the value of 2705 articles at tenpence each
Ansr. £112 - 14 - 2

If 36 men earn £9 -6 -4½ what money can 246 men earn   Ansr. £65 -4 -7½

What is the value of 54 ac. 1 rood 18 po. at £62 -10 -9 per acre   Ansr. £3399 -13 -10 ⁷⁄₈₀ d

And all of this without calculators! Typically, Standard 5 would be 11- or 12-year-old children and they needed to handle matters like conversions between acres, rods and perches – as in the last calculation above.

Just a couple of example "testers" from the same source that the reader might care to try: -

- If a servant's wages be £25 a year, what would he receive for 87 days service? (Expressed in pounds, shillings, pence and farthings.)
- If 17cwt 3qrs 14lbs of tallow cost £38 -2s -8d, how much may be bought for £5 -12s -6d at the same rate? (Expressed in cwt, qrs, lbs and ounces.)

On 16th January 1878, the Government issued a circular to all of Her Majesty's Inspectors of Schools[64]. The document sets out the Government's expectations for elementary education and some extracts are very relevant to "teaching the Heathens": -

"...to promote the development of the general intelligence of the Scholars rather than to seek to burden their memories with subjects which... would not likely to be of use to them."

"...endeavour to provide that all children... shall at least have acquired the power of writing with facility, of using the simple rules of arithmetic without difficulty and of reading without exertion and with pleasure to themselves."

"...attention should be specially directed to the interesting stories of History, to the lives of noble characters and to incidents which create a patriotic feeling of regard for their Country..."

So, indeed, a momentous year for the new school: -

- A brand-new building.
- A pupil intake of about ninety children.
- The successful joining together of the new C.E. school with Reading's Methodist school and the continuing teaching contribution from William Reading.
- Two formal inspections by an Education Authority and a Diocesan Authority inspector with very complimentary reports.
- Many visits by supporters including the Augustas – mother and daughter – the clergy – the Rector and Curate and local landowners including the Aldridge's.
- Gifts of equipment and books to the school from the Bigg family and a Bigg family school treat.

It could not really have been a better start.

---

64 Government Circular to HM Inspectors of Schools.

Chapter 16

1884/5 – The Second Academic Year – *and what a difference*

The school reopened on 1st September after what Annie Farrer (Head Teacher) describes as the "Harvest Holidays". Mr Scrase, the Education Authority Attendance Officer, called several times because of the high number of absences for hop picking and acorn picking. The reference to the Harvest – as opposed to Summer holiday – and the absences for hop picking and other activities show that the year still revolved around seasonal and agricultural events and that the children, as wage earners, were still important contributors to the family income.

However, the Log Book (ref. 1) entry for 29th September is a startling one. It reads: -

"On account of the continual abuse and persecution I am subject to from some of the parents, I have, this day, sent in my resignation to the Rector *(in his capacity as Chairman of the school managers)*. 3 months' notice. A Farrer. Mistress".

There are no signs anywhere – Augusta's diaries, earlier log book entries, Inspectors reports – that this problem existed. However, there is a hint that all may not have been well in log book references to minor pilfering taking place in October.

The first term ended on 19th December with a "treat and prizes" for the pupils. And Annie Farrer "Resigned charge of the school on this date". The record shows (Appendix 3) that Annie moved to teach in Wiltshire after leaving her Mannings Heath post. On the face of it, it seems a shame that events turned out as they did because Annie did sterling work to get the new school up and running. It may be that things got out of hand due to the illness of the Rector, who was Chairman of the school Management Committee. He was ill[65] through

---

65 Ruri-Decanal Parish Magazine.

November and December, so not in a position to deal with the issues underpinning the abuse that Annie suffered.

The school reopened, after the Christmas Holiday, on 12th January, with William Reading in charge for the first two weeks of the term.

On 26th January, Annie Harwood took over as Head Teacher. She moved to Mannings Heath from a teaching post in Doncaster. She was young, about 26 years old and a certificated teacher, so Mannings Heath was a promotion for her as a Head Teacher (see Appendix 3). Ref. 65 for February, 1885, records the appointment of Annie Harwood and also that two concerts were held to raise funds for a porch on the South side of the school.

Augusta, in her diary entry for 3rd February, tells us that she went to the school and listened to Annie Harwood teaching grammar. She "thought it clear and painstaking but she *(Annie)* has little to say in favour of the poor children who are *(in the view of Annie)* 'dirty, backward and have little mind'". Annie Harwood's log book entry for the same event says that she found the grammar "most defective throughout the school".

This is not the only reference to Annie Harwood's expressed view of the inadequacies of her charges. On 12th February, she records the Standard IV reading was "very defective". In April, she records that none of the Standards are able to do the needlework for that Standard and that she needed to devote much effort to improving the level of ability throughout the school. Also in April, she records that "School upset on account of the dirty habits of a little girl". This was repeated on the next day and the child sent home. On 20th May, Annie examined Standard IV in grammar and "found them very stupid" and, on the following day "very slow in replying to the questions in grammar".

Throughout the year there were continuing concerns about attendance with many references to low numbers attending school. Sometimes the log book gives reasons but, on many occasions, it is just a statement like "Attendance poor". On 16th and 17th February, poor attendance was attributed to wet weather. 1st May was not a school holiday but attendance was poor because pupils took a Mayday holiday off their own bat. The day after the Whit Monday holiday was also poor in attendance. On 8th June, there were only fifty-eight pupils present out of a total complement of about seventy-five and, on 15th June, it was even worse, with just fifty-four pupils present. On 6th August, the log book records that "Only a very few children at school being the annual school treat belonging to the Chapel". This presumably refers to the Sunday School taking place in the first Methodist Chapel. The "treat" was, in fact, a visit to The Hyde, which was

Chapter 16: 1884/5 – The Second Academic Year –*and what a difference*

the residence of a Bigg family relative. Does this reflect a continuing allegiance to the "old ways" of Readings, the Methodist school, or was it just one of finding an excuse not to go to school? Either way, it made life difficult for Annie Harwood.

Annie, as Head Teacher, was clearly upset by many instances where the smooth running of the school was disturbed by what she felt were "peripheral" activities. In February, she records that "The children taken to Church at 11.30. Find it disturbs the school very much". In April, she records that the school was made "disorderly" by an entertainment being given. Augusta, in her diary tells us that this was two plays and the Parish Magazine records the entertainment as being stage managed by William Reading. In May, Annie records that "the whole of the afternoon's work was interrupted" by a visit to Church. She made her concerns known to Augusta who records in her diary that "…Miss Harwood brought the children *(to the Church)*, though complaining it interrupts School".

The first signs of difficulties between Annie Harwood and William Reading began to appear in March when Augusta records in her diary that she spoke with William about clashes between the two with William "doing things that she refused to do", thus weakening the authority of the Head Teacher. Earlier in that month, when Augusta took Annie to Horsham, Annie told Augusta that "… she thought Mr Reading was leading a <u>bad life</u> with Mrs Wilkins – so Mrs Tampkin told her! It much surprised and distressed me…". Small village scuttle butt at its best, but it held the signs of things to come.

But this was not the only clash that Annie had with the "locals". On 8th June, Rev McCarogher "Visited the school and read out the names of the children who had passed the different standards". Annie, as the Head Teacher, objected strongly. Rev McCarogher writes in the log book, "To this, the Mistress objected, denying me my right as Manager of the school to do so". Annie then adds her objections to the log book entry because she felt strongly that announcing the standards achieved by her charges was part of her responsibilities.

Matters came to an explosive head on 24th June when the log book entry, by Annie Harwood, reads "The assistant Master has taken the Head Mistresses place, ordered the children to <u>disobey</u> and if she <u>enforces</u> her <u>orders</u> to <u>kick</u> her. Came into school this afternoon found the school assembled. Ordered the girls to come into the classroom; the assistant *(William Reading)* ordered them to sit still and they came into the room. He called me a she… *(word blacked out in the log book)*. The Rev McCarogher visited to enquire into the above and read a letter Mr Reading had written. Mr Reading offered an apology before all the children for his conduct".

As one would expect, Augusta became involved in the matter. In her diary, she writes "Rebellion at A. Harwood's school! Two despatches sent to me before 10 am! And when I went down found Mr Reading Master of the school, Mrs Harwood outside with her pupils! She had written to Mr McC and so had he. He had called her names before the children and told the boys to kick her! I spoke to Reading privately and did not like his attitude. I could do nothing and went off to Church. Most oppressive."

The next day, the 25th June, Augusta went into the school and did not know what to expect. However, she found that normal prayers had been said and a Bible lesson was in progress, but under the charge of the Curate. Augusta records that "Mr Reading behaving very badly and rude to me so I left and wrote to Committee, sending letter to Mr McC who wrote back kindly."

This must all have been very upsetting for Augusta, and quite uncharacteristic behaviour from William Reading. Augusta had put so much of herself into the school and in support of William Reading and she clearly feared it was all to turn to ashes. There are no clear-cut reasons for William's outburst and behaviour except, possibly, he was at odds with the views expressed by Annie Harwood about the children, and her seeming not to really "fit in" to the community. Maybe, too, there was a frustration because he felt he could do a better job himself than was being done. Maybe there is a clue in the Inspector's report described below.

Despite the apology from William, the matter was not ended and Annie continues to write in the log book about the work of the school being interrupted "…with Mr Reading's continual quarrelling".

As an interesting aside on this event, someone, in a very different hand, has written in the log book, following the reference to William's apology, the Latin phrase "Audi alteram partem" which means "listen to the other side". We do not know who wrote this but I suspect it may have been Rev McCarogher.

Before the "explosion", the school was subject to an inspection by the Education Authority Inspector, George French, on 27th May. George French had also made the inspection in 1884, in the first school year, when he was, in general, very complementary about what had been achieved. This time, however, it was different. He was very critical of the standard of reading, to the point where he threatened to fine the school for not performing if there was not a big improvement at the next inspection. He was also very critical of the handwriting, the repetitions and the spelling. In the Infant class, he was critical of the singing but did record an improvement in handwriting and arithmetic. He wanted to see

Chapter 16: 1884/5 – The Second Academic Year –and what a difference

better pictures on the walls and to be able to witness good conversations about common objects.

All in all, this was not a good report and clearly identified matters needing attention.

Whilst all this was going on, Augusta was continuing her efforts to get a house built, on the land adjacent to the school that had been given by Charles Scrase Dickins, as accommodation for the school Head Teacher. Her diary records that she would give £200 to pay for the construction and, after much toing and froing, settled on a quotation of £194 from Edwin Leppard and, she records, with obvious joy, "…to begin at once" at the beginning of July.

The Parish Magazine for June gave thanks for the progress made in these terms. "The munificent gift of £200 has been made by Miss Bigg towards the building of a School House and Mr Scrase Dickins has, with great liberality, given the site. May a blessing attend their generosity."

Annie Harwood had already handed in her resignation as Head Teacher and left the school at the end of the Summer term on 14th August. Ultimately, she returned to her home county of Yorkshire to continue her teaching career.

So, this second year had been a starkly disappointing follow-on to the very successful first year. We had: -

- A Head Teacher seemingly at odds with the society in which she was working and with a very "downbeat" view of her charges.
- Consequences in the form of absenteeism, some petty pilfering and falling educational standards.
- Very uncharacteristic behaviour from William Reading.

The two good bits were that Augusta continued her support for the school and managed to have a start made on the School House – so, perhaps, not all bad in the end.

Chapter 17

September 1885/April 1887, The Third Academic Year – and the arrival and departure of Louisa Buck

The third academic year started on 21st September 1885, with sixty-eight pupils on the register (ref. 1). It was also the day that Louisa Buck took over as Head following the resignation of Annie Harwood. In Chapter 9, the romantic relationship with William Reading is described, which resulted in Miss Louisa Buck becoming Mrs Louisa Reading.

Louisa's first entry in the log book (Ref. 1) is the very formal "I, Louisa Buck, took charge of the school today, 53 children present". Absenteeism was clearly a continuing problem – sixty-eight on the register and only fifty-three attending.

On this first day, Louisa took the children to Church at 11.15 and Augusta writes in her diary that "Miss Buck and Mr Reading brought the children. *(This was, presumably, to the Mission Church, as it was then called, built by the Biggs in Mannings Heath; now known as the Church of the Good Shepherd.)* It was quite a new service to them. Not many communicants."

On 2nd October, Louisa shows her determination to raise the standard being achieved in English. This confirms her response to some of the concerns expressed by the Inspector in May 1885. She took strong and immediate action by identifying the poetry to be studied.

For Standard I - "The Pin" by Ella Wilcox, who was an American poet at the height of her career in the second half of the 19th century.

For Standards II and III - "The Use of Sight" from the collection of Original Poems published in 1836.

Also, for Standard III - "The Captain's Daughter" by James Thomas Fields; another American poet at the height of his powers in the mid-19th century.

For Standards IV and V - "Bishop Hatto, God's Judgement on a Wicked Bishop" by Robert Southey 1774-1843; an English poet of the Romantic school.

For Standard V – King Henry's Address before Agincourt (the St Crispen's Day speech by William Shakespeare).

For Standard VI – "The Battle of Blenheim"; another poem by Robert Southey.

These are all challenging and demanding works for elementary school pupils and their selection is a clear glimpse into the professionalism of Louisa as a teacher and her determination to raise the standard of learning amongst "the Heathens".

Then came the bombshell.

In her diary for 31st December, Augusta records that "Mr McC *(the Rector John McCarogher)* gave out that our excellent Miss Buck was leaving for a better appointment. She has improved the school wonderfully".

The Parish Magazine (Ref 65) provides the formal record: -

"Miss Buck, who has been the Schoolmistress at Mannings Heath for the past three months, has sent in her resignation, having obtained a post of mistress in an orphanage at Bristol. During the short time she has been amongst us, she has effected a very great improvement in the school; the behaviour and general appearance of the children presenting a striking contrast to that of a few weeks ago. We all part with her with most sincere regret, and heartily wish her every success in her new and enlarged sphere of work."

Louisa makes no reference to her resignation in the School Log Book (Ref 1) but she had obviously made a very big impact in a short time – on the children and parents, and on William Reading (see Chapter 10), as we will see in May 1887.

In November, there was an inspection of the school by the Diocesan Inspector, George Heath. A very good report, except for concerns about the knowledge of the catechism.

There were continuing problems of absence. There were over seventy pupils on the school register but, for example, in November an average of fifty-four were present, but in the first week of December, this had fallen to forty-four and, in the week before Christmas, to forty-two. In early January 1886, there was a further fall to a weekly average of thirty-six. Some of this was due to sickness and, in January, to deep snow, but nevertheless, attendance remained an issue. In February, the school closed for two weeks because of an outbreak of scarlet fever.

It was on 15th February that Louisa recorded her departure with the short sentence, "I resign charge of the school".

Rosina Williams was appointed as the School Mistress and re-opened the school in March, after the scarlet fever outbreak had reduced in severity. Rosina became the first occupant of the newly completed School House.

Scarlet fever was followed, in March, by an outbreak of measles with many absences – only sixteen children at school on 1st April. The school did not re-open until April 26th with forty-two present.

There was concern for the school expressed in the Parish Magazine for May as "Miss Williams is consequently beginning her duties under difficulties; we can only hope that due allowances *[presumably by the Education and Diocesan inspectors]* will be made for the many drawbacks....".

The one positive was the hope, expressed by the Parish Council, that "Miss Cooper's little school...." can become united with the main Mannings Heath School (see Chapter 11). In fact, this did happen on 26th July when Fanny Cooper joined the staff of Mannings Heath School and brought her eight pupils to transfer to the school as well.

The May Parish Magazine contains a financial report for the combined Nuthurst and Mannings Heath schools *[combined because there was just one Management Committee looking after both schools and they were both within the Parish of Nuthurst]*. The accounts show an annual cost for both schools of just over £300 for the year, covered by an income of about £140 from government payments and the remaining £160 being funded by donations (£130) and a "voluntary" rate at 6d yielding the remaining £30.

It is clear that some of the promised donations and "voluntary" rate payments were slow in coming forward. The consequences were that the teachers were owed reimbursement to the tune of about £55. The Rector recorded that, "It was a great and undeserved hardship that the teachers should be kept without their salaries". *[Just imagine the furore that would erupt if that happened today!]*

The school was inspected by the Diocesan Inspector on 22nd July and he seems, in his report, to have made some allowances for the initial "difficulties" attending the resignation of Louisa Buck, a new Mistress and the school closures due to sickness. A reasonable grant of nearly £35 was forthcoming, which the Rector felt was "...as favourable as could be expected under adverse circumstances".

Chapter 17: *September 1885/April 1887,* The Third Academic Year

However, trouble was looming on the horizon.

The School Attendance Officer called to see Rosina about her refusal to admit Claude Worcester into the school. Rosina told him that it was because his mother kept him at home at playtime and would not allow him to return, causing Rosina to have to remove his entry from the register for that day. Rosina asked Claude's mother to accompany Claude to the school *[presumably so that she could discuss the action with her]* but Claude's mother refused.

This is one of those "stand-off" incidents that can get out of hand - and this one did.

The Managers Committee considered the matter and instructed Rosina to admit Claude but she refused and was suspended from her role on 11th January. The matter was then referred, by the Managers, to the Education Department and, if Rosina is to be believed, the Rector refused to tell her what they concluded, but proceeded to dismiss her without notice.

Not only that but Rosina had to get out of the School House, of which she was the first occupant, by 29th January – just over two weeks after being given notice.

What a mess – the roller coaster of the first years of the school continued! A temporary Mistress was appointed for three months and, on 14th February, Miss Turner took up her duties as Mistress on a three-month temporary contract.

The school inspection carried out in July had shown a lack of desks and, as usual, Augusta Bigg came to the rescue and donated the additional desks and forms the Inspector identified as necessary. The Rector, in the Parish Magazine formally recorded thanks and Augusta's "usual liberality".

Despite the difficulties, Augusta remains steadfast in her support for the school with frequent visits, numerous small gifts and coming to the rescue with the additional desks. So not all bad, but hardly a stable platform for the future.

Chapter 18

May 1887/May 1913, The Return of Louisa – *and real progress*

We have no documentary evidence as to why Louisa Buck returned to Mannings Heath, to marry William Reading and to resume her position of Mistress of the school. On the face of it, it appears to have been an unlikely set of events.

- How did William manage his courtship of Louisa with him in Mannings Heath and she in Bristol?
- Why did she give up her promotion to return to a small, elementary school?
- Why did Rosina Williams appear to "lose the plot" over a simple disciplinary matter and thus lose her job?
- Why did Rev John McCarogher behave in such an uncharacteristic manner in his dealings with Rosina and her dismissal?

Many questions and no evidence to provide answers, so perhaps we can enjoy the luxury of a little speculation. Perhaps the "pull" of love and the availability of a nice house, the School House, served to provide for a motive for the "Heathens" to find a reason for Rosina Williams to lose the position of Mannings Heath School Mistress and to pave the way for the return of Louisa? We do not know for sure but just perhaps there was a sub-plot being played out between Louisa Buck leaving in February 1886 and returning as Louisa Reading in May 1887.

However, it all came about, as reported in Chapter 10, Louisa and William married at St Andrew's Church, Nuthurst, on 24th April and, after what must have been a very short honeymoon, Louisa records in the Log Book on 9th May that "I, Louisa Reading, took charge of the school today".

One of the immediate results of Louisa's return was a dramatic improvement in attendance to an average of sixty-five (out of the seventy on the register).

Perhaps the best way to gain a picture of life in the school is to use the words that Louisa wrote in her Log Book for a "typical" year. The mid-point of Louisa's tenure as School Mistress was the year 1900 and her record for that year is shown below. In that year, there were about eighty pupils on the register. However, there is some doubt about the complete accuracy of numbers taken from the register. It seems as though a head count from the register entrants and leavers leads to an overstatement of numbers. It is likely that a more valid number of pupils would be nearer to sixty than eighty.

'Feb 2   An infant admitted.

 9   Miss Cooper was absent on Monday and Tuesday; not well. The Rector visited on Tuesday, and Miss Bigg on Friday. (This is more evidence of the long term and continuing support that Augusta Bigg gave to the school.)

 16   On Wednesday morning, the very small attendance prevented keeping school. Thursday morning was as bad and, at midday, the children were sent home as the road (presumably Golding Lane.) was becoming impassable with water. Poor attendance all the week, much snow and rain.

 19   I examined the infants to-day. Their attainments are scarcely equal to the syllabus, their attendances for the last period (two months) has been irregular on account of severe weather.

 27   Altered the opening of afternoon school from 1.30 to 2.0

'Mar 2   Mr Brooks called.   (Mr Brooks was the Education Authority Attendance Officer.)

   Miss Bigg and another lady visited the school this afternoon. The elder children have been examined this week.

 23   'Jan 1

 26   5

 30   12

'April 2   19

 3   22

 9   26

 12   Closed for Easter holiday. 6 children still absent.

	23	Re- opened. 51 present, 5 reported ill. Mr Brooks called.
	26	Checked the register and found the attendances correctly entered. GK Boyd. (G.K. Boyd is the Rector, having succeeded John MaCarogher, and is Chairman of the Management Committee. One of his responsibilities is to carry out regular register checks.}
	29	The children have had their periodical examination this week.
'May	1	Began the new school year. Moved the children into new standards. (See Chapter 15 for details of the Standard 1 to Standard 6 requirements.) All those who are over six years old are placed in Standard 1 but John Cox, only recently admitted, and Allen Ansell, a delicate child, are retained in the infant class. 7 children absent on account of illness. 13 have made perfect attendances this quarter, and 8 in the year.
	2	Two of the absentees returned this morning.
	16	Mr Brooks called.
	21	All the children present to-day except three of the eldest. One of them is in hospital. An infant admitted.
	25	Checked register and found attendances correctly entered. GK Boyd. Holiday on Thursday as it was Ascension Day.
	28	Admitted a boy; a visitor to the village.
	31	Closed the school for Whitsuntide.
'June	11	Re-opened with a good attendance.
	13	Received the Scheme of Work approved by HMI (The Education Authority Inspectorate.) The Scheme of Work, described in the Log Book, is very detailed but, in summary, covers from Standard 1 to Standard 6 and includes: -

- English reading, writing and grammar.
- Recitation of poems and poetry created by pupils.

- Arithmetic – as described in Chapter 15.
- Geography – local and England as a whole.
- History of the Stuart period.
- Common things – insects, plants and animals.
- Elementary Science – agricultural and domestic.
- Singing
- Drawing
- Needlework
- Physical exercise – dumb bell drills.
- Object Lessons

'July 4 — Admitted an infant. Number on books is higher than for some time.

5 — Holiday in the afternoon, Mr Reading being absent at an inquest.

17 — Holiday in the afternoon, that the teachers and some of the elder girls might attend the GFS festival.

19 — Mr Brooks called.

20 — Drill has been let alone for the past fortnight on account of the excessive heat.

27 — The new time-table has been used this week.

'Aug 1 — Miss Bigg visited the school this morning.

2 — The children have had their periodical examination and were dismissed for their holiday today at noon. Two children, visitors, have left.

Summary of the HMI Report.

"A satisfactory start has been made with the teaching of singing by note and the work generally appeared to be up to the usual standard though there is room for improvement in the teaching of word building in the infant's class.

FE Cooper is continued under Article 68 of the Code.

Louisa Reading, Mistress

Fanny E Cooper, Additional Teacher for Infants

GK Boyd, Correspondent

(As a result of the inspection, the school received £64.13s.6d from the Education Authority, plus an Aid Grant of £40 for a new window and improved ventilation. As a bonus, it was sanctioned that the annual inspection would not need to take place. This is a splendid result for all Louisa's efforts.)

'Sep 3	Re-opened, 54 children present. 5 withdrawn, 1 reported ill and 3 others away for holiday.
4	Mr Brooks visited the school and looked at the register.
10	Miss Cooper absent today. Admitted three children (visitors).
20	Checked registers and found attendances correctly entered. GK Boyd
26	Received notice of the Diocesan Inspection. Sent C Stoner to Horsham to be examined for a Labour Certificate.
'Oct 4	Three children withdrawn.
9	Miss Biggs and Miss Curtis visited the school.
11	Diocesan Inspection by the Rev G Heath. There were present the Revs GH Boyd and Elaughlin and 58 children. An elder boy withdrawn.
23	Miss MaCaragher visited the school this morning and saw the children drill.
'Nov 2	School working as usual. The attendances keeping very good in spite of some very wet days; except for Rose Brister, one of the elder girls who neither attends nor leaves. She has not attended since the Diocesan Inspection.
12	Commenced the winter time for afternoon school 1.30 to 3.45.
14	Received the Diocesan Report.
26	Gave a lesson on the Mole instead of on Friday to take advantage of using a real specimen.

Chapter 18: May 1887/May 1913, The Return of Louisa – *and real progress*

Report of Religious Instruction.

I am glad to be able to report a marked improvement in Religious Knowledge. The answering was very creditable in all the groups. That of the senior group was especially intelligent and general.

George Heath – Diocesan Inspector

27	The Rector gave the children their Diocesan Certificates.
30	The school was closed to-day for the opening of the C.L.B. Drill Hall.
'Dec 3	During this month, we propose to devote more time to arithmetic in the upper class than is shown on the timetable.
14	I have examined the Infants this week. Their work shows improvement. Writing and drawing are alike weak and wavering.
20	The Rector distributed the medals and prizes for attendance to the children.
21	Dismissed the children for a fortnight holiday

During the tenure of Louisa as Mistress, we have five school photographs taken in 1898, 1902, 1905, 1906 and 1909. Unfortunately, we only have the names of a few of the children but, never the less, the photographs show the changes in style of photograph and dress over the period from 1898 to 1909.

1898

Back row, 1st left – William George Glasher (aged 6)
Front row, 2nd right – Fred Morton Glaysher (aged 3)

1902

Back row, 4th left – William George Glaysher (aged 10)
2nd row, 4th left - Fred Morton Glaysher (aged 7)
Front row, 4th left – John James Glaysher (aged 5)

1905

Back row, 3rd left – Billy Richardson (aged 11)
Second row, 1st left – Bill Thorns (aged 4)
Second row, 2nd left – Ernest Thorns
Front row, 3rd left – Edith Annie Mary (May) Ansell (aged 6)

Chapter 18: May 1887/May 1913, The Return of Louisa – *and real progress*

1906

Back row, 3rd left – Fred Morton Glaysher (aged 11)
2nd row, 1st left – John James Glaysher (aged 9)

1909

Back row, 1st left – John James Glaysher (aged 12)
2nd row, 3rd left – Ronald Alfred Glaysher (aged 9)

(Notice that the pupils are all wearing their medals awarded as a result of success in various examinations, including their Religious Knowledge tested at the annual inspection by the Diocesan Inspector.)

During Louisa's twenty-six years as the Mannings Heath School Mistress there were many developments in the education of the local young people. In this part of the story, I will attempt to summarise the most significant of these.

The 1870 Act made it obligatory for Elementary education to be provided by local authorities but what it did not do was make attendance at elementary schools to be compulsory. The 1880 Elementary Education Act made elementary education compulsory until the age of 10. (*This "age of 10" will have a real significance for Mannings Heath School when we reach the 1920s*). Under the 1880 Act, a person shall not take into employment any child who is under the age of 10. Between the ages of 10 and 13, employment can be given providing the child has met the Labour Certificate requirements in reading, writing and elementary arithmetic, having attended a "certified, efficient school". (*It could be that it was the wording of the 1880 Act that contributed to the emphasis on "efficiency" in the local authority correspondence leading to a school in Mannings Heath - see Chapter 13*).

Poverty, leading to the inability to pay the attendance fee at an elementary school was not a excuse. It became an obligation on the parish to pay the fee ensuring that the child received education. There is evidence in the log book of this being applied to the Highgate children (Alfred, Thomas and William) early in the life of the school. They were the children of Alfred Highgate who was an agricultural labourer, with five children, living in a cottage at Hammer Pond.

So, the shift we see is a movement to make elementary education the "norm" rather than a "take it or leave it" way of life.

However, the 1880 Act did not overcome all the attendance issues and it still took a considerable effort – both insistence and persuasion – to achieve consistently high levels of attendance to give continuity of education and to create rising standards of achievement.

Bouts of illness and sickness were a continual problem and led to poor attendance and, in some cases, complete closure of the school. These bouts were mostly, but not always, in the winter months and some examples are: -

- February 1888 – colds and sore throats.
- June and July 1889 – measles outbreak closed the school.
- November and December 1889 – outbreak of mumps.
- February 1890 – influenza outbreak affected teachers and pupils and closed the school.

- February and October 1892 – coughs and sickness led to very reduced attendance.
- September 1893 and October 1894 – unspecified illness led to reduced attendance.
- February 1897 – colds and influenza outbreak.
- May 1901 – measles outbreak.
- August and September 1901 – "eruptions" on hands and faces meant that many children had to be sent home.
- April 1902 – eye infections.
- January 1903 – whooping cough outbreak.
- July 1907 – mumps outbreak closed the school.
- October 1907 – measles outbreak closed the school.
- September 1909 – reported cases of diphtheria.
- July 1910 – Medical Officer excluded 26 children with coughs and closed the school.

The weather was also a cause of poor levels of attendance, with snow and heavy rain being the main culprits. Heavy snow and impassable roads closed the school in February 1888, February and March 1889, and January and February 1901. Wet weather and flooding also reduced numbers in July 1888, and in most years up to 1901.

It is interesting to note that weather did not seem to have any recorded effect on attendance after 1901. This may well come from there being a growing acceptance that school attendance was the norm and beneficial, so parents tried harder to ensure their children were regular attenders. Therefore, more to do with societal changes in attitude than improvements in the climate.

There were a number of social events and seasonal activities, with Mannings Heath as an agricultural community, that impacted regular attendance. Some of those, recorded by Louisa, are: -

- Stag hound meets in February.
- Garland making and carrying to celebrate May Day.
- The Band of Hope festival and galas in Horsham and at Crabtree in July.
- Wesleyan and Nuthurst Sunday School treats in July and August.
- The hay harvest usually in July which, along with hop picking in September and October, provided opportunities for the children to earn money for their families.
- Recorded, but not each year, were substantial absences for acorn picking (probably as food for the family pig), blackberrying and fishing in September and beating for shooting in October.

But again, we see a fall in such events impacting on attendance as the period of Louisa's tenure goes on and, by the time we get to 1910, it is really only things like the Sunday School treats that are impacting recorded attendance.

Louisa made significant personal efforts to improve attendance and this was also part of the role of the Education Authority and, latterly, the West Sussex Education Committee.

Among those efforts were: -

- Regular, often monthly, visits by the Attendance Officer, to check on attendance and the register.
- Personal notes written by Louisa to parents to urge and cajole for regular attendance.
- In his capacity as Chairman of the Managers, regular checks by Rev McCarogher on the correctness of attendance records in the school register.
- After 1903, the introduction of half day holidays as a reward for good attendance. From the records, it looks as though over 90% attendance by the entire school pupils for the month would earn a holiday reward.
- The award of medals and certificates to individual pupils for good attendance.
- The growing award of Labour Certificates that enabled children to obtain paid employment at 12 or 13 years of age, providing they had reached the required level of learning which, of course, only came from regular school attendance.

Gradually, these efforts were rewarded and, by the end of Louisa's tenure in 1913, we are seeing regular attendance levels of over 95% for each month and the regular award of the half day holiday.

However, these "carrot" efforts were supported by legal enforcement. There is a report in the Sussex Agricultural Express of 5th March 1889, of Pharoah Blackwell of Nuthurst (Mill Farm Cottage) being summoned for employing a child under age. The child was his son, James, who was one of Pharoah's five children. James had been a pupil at Readings School and had joined Mannings Heath School in October 1883 along with other Reading's pupils. The case against Pharoah was made by John Scrase who was the Attendance Officer responsible for Mannings Heath School. He claimed that James had been absent from school thirty-two times during the previous eight weeks up to 8th February. James had been employed to look after sheep and therefore not able to attend school regularly, his mother claimed. The result was that Pharoah was fined 1s. James left school in November aged 13 having achieved only Standard 1, so would not have qualified for a Labour Certificate. The census

Chapter 18: May 1887/May 1913, The Return of Louisa – *and real progress*

records indicate that James continued as an agricultural labourer after leaving school.

The period from 1887 to 1913 saw major changes in the running and operation of Mannings Heath School. These same changes would have been present in all the local authority elementary and C.E. schools within West Sussex, and coming under the West Sussex Education Committee.

In 1883, the involvement of the authorities in the operation of the school consisted of: -

- A Management Committee chaired by the Rector of Nuthurst.
- Regular, usually monthly, visits from the Attendance Officer.
- Inspections every year by the Diocesan Inspector.
- Inspections every year by Her Majesty's Inspector.

In 1902, there was a further Education Act, known as the Balfour Act. Its consequences for the governance of elementary education were considerable. The Act provided funds for religious instruction in elementary schools, C of E and Roman Catholic. It set the route for transferring the role of School Boards to local borough or county councils, and for the formation of Local Education Authorities (LEAs) and Education Committees with powers to develop the existing system of elementary schools.

A consequence for Nuthurst and Mannings Hath was that a new school Management Committee had to be established. So, in May 1903, the new committee to manage Nuthurst and Mannings Heath schools was constituted as: -

Rev. G.K. Boyd (Rector of Nuthurst) – Chairman
Edwin Leppard – representing the County Council
G.H. Gander – representing the Parish Council
C.R. Scrase Dickins, Col. Olivant and Major Bigg – ordinary members.

By 1913, the involvement had developed to: -

- A Management Committee chaired by the Rector of Nuthurst.
- Regular, usually monthly, visits from the Attendance Officer.
- Inspections every year by the Diocesan Inspector.
- Inspections every year by His Majesty's Inspector.
- Medical examinations carried out by nurses and the appointed Medical Officer who had the authority to close the school.
- Visits by the Education Authority Physical Training Instructors to set up and

supervise drill and PE activities.
- Education Authority set schemes of work for each year.

On this administrative front, it is interesting to compare the salaries being paid to the teaching staff.

In 1908, Louisa, as the Head, was paid £105 per annum and William, her husband, classified as an Assistant Teacher because he did not hold a teaching qualification, was paid only £45 per annum. Fanny Cooper, also classified as an Assistant Teacher, and the person who brought her "little school" into the Mannings Heath School (see Chapter 11), was paid a little less at £42 per annum.

Reference 65 – the Parish Magazine – contains a number of items concerning Mannings Heath School through 1887 to 1900.

The entry for July 1887, records that all the school children were presented with a medal, in the form of a Maltese Cross, by the Rector in memory of Queen Victoria's jubilee. Mrs Augusta Bigg funded entertainment for the children in the Rectory grounds for those in Nuthurst and at Mannings Heath School after a service in the Mission Church (*now known as the Church of the Good Shepherd or, less formally, as the Little Church*). It also records that Miss Augusta Bigg presented a large number of interesting books to the people of Mannings Heath and the Readings would house the books at School House and give them out, as a library, on the first Saturday of each month.

In September 1887, the Mannings Heath School classroom was doubled in size thanks to the generosity of Miss Augusta. This matter of overcrowding had been mentioned in the Inspector's reports and this increase in class room size addressed the concern.

It is not mentioned in the Mannings Heath School log books but the Parish Magazine mentions the establishment of evening classes in October 1887. Other entries indicate that the teaching is done by the Readings in Mannings Heath and this is, presumably, an attempt to make education available to the older generation.

In November 1890, there is a record of Louisa returning from St Bartholomew's Hospital after treatment. The note says that she "much benefited, though not, we fear cured by the treatment she has been under". One suspects that this may be the first reference to the uterine cancer from which she died shortly after retirement.

September saw a major Parish event – the death of the Rector, the Rev. John Ommanney McCarogher, aged 64 on 12th September 1891, and his burial on 17th September. The funeral service at St Andrew's Church was attended by a huge congregation. The children from Mannings Heath School gave a floral tribute and many, with their parents, attended the service as observers and participants.

The long tribute in the Parish magazine contains the following summary of a little of what he achieved. "He found it *(the Parish of Nuthurst)* disorganised, neglected, broken into jarring fragments, schoolless *(although as earlier Chapters show, this is not a wholly complete picture),* with a dilapidated Church. He leaves it with a restored Church, new rectory, two sets of Schools and teachers' houses, two mission Churches, frequent services well attended, and a harmonious population, united in peace and fellowship…"

His grave is to the south of the Church in line with the main, south door entrance. It carries the inscription "JOHN OMMANNEY M'CAROGHER, priest. Born 12th September, 1826. At rest 12th September, 1891"

The grave of Rev. John McCarogher, St Andrew's, Nuthurst.

In February 1892, the successor to Rev. McCarogher, Rev George Boyd, was inducted and took over the role of Chairman of the Mannings Heath School Managers.

In May 1893, the Mannings Heath School inspection by Mr Garland, the Assistant HMI, went very well. The improved condition of the building and new furniture contributed to this success. On the academic side, only one pupil put forward for the Standard 4 examination had failed, compared with four failures from Nuthurst. The general rating, for grant payment purposes, was Good.

July 1894 saw the completion of the upgrading work at Mannings Heath School. Reports from HMI recorded that the school was now in highly satisfactory state and, academically, was reported as having "gained ground" since the last inspection.

On a lighter note, we also see in May 1910, that Summer games were being played. Louisa records that cricket and stool ball commenced in May. We have records of two cricket matches, one versus Lower Beeding School on 26th June 1909 and one versus Roffey School on 9th September, 1911. In the 1909 match, Mannings Heath players were Fred Richardson, Charley Jupp, Picton Highgate, Wallace Worcester, Leslie Worcester, Allan Ansell, Robert Gatland, Arthur Simpson, George Jones, Charles Mitchell and Cecil Mitchell. Mannings Heath scored a total of sixty-nine from two innings with Fred Richardson making a total of thirty-three. Mannings Heath won by four wickets. The match against Roffey was not such a happy affair for Mannings Heath. They were all out for twenty-five when facing a Roffey total of one hundred and twenty – so a heavy loss. The Roffey "star" was WF Lanaway who made sixty-four runs and took five Mannings Heath wickets.

Both matches were reported in the West Sussex County Times.

Numbers on the school register fluctuated throughout Louisa's tenure. In 1887 there were about eighty pupils, which had fallen to about fifty-five in 1890, but risen again to seventy in 1892. In 1896, there were sixty-one on the register and this stayed fairly constant through to 1899. In 1903, this had risen to sixty-nine and stayed around or over sixty up to 1910. Thereafter, there was a gradual decline to forty-three in 1913.

Louisa's last entry in the log book, for 9th May 1913, reads "The children were dismissed for a week's holiday (Whit week) after which I resign the charge of the school. 43 children on the books. Percentage (attendance) for the week 97.5. *Louisa Reading.*"

Chapter 18: May 1887/May 1913, The Return of Louisa – *and real progress*

A typically quiet, low key and professional departure of a fine school mistress who had done much to raise the standards and to shape the future of the school and the 400 plus children admitted during her 26-year tenure.

Louisa and William both retired at the same time and left the School House to live in The Bungalow, next door to the Mission Church (Church of the Good Shepherd as it is known today).

Sadly, Louisa died on 16th September 1913, after just four short months of retirement. She died from cancer of the uterus which was probably what took her to St Bartholomew's Hospital in 1890.

William continued living at The Bungalow until November 1913 when he sold, by auction, most of the household furniture and outdoor effects, before moving into his brother's house Hillbrow (now known as Igls) opposite the Dun Horse pub. Louisa was buried at St Andrew's, Nuthurst, and the grave is opposite the south door of the church. William died in 1937 and is buried alongside Louisa. The grave bears the following: -

"In loving memory of Louisa. Wife of William Reading. Born May 17th 1848. Died September 16th 1913. There remaineth rest to the people of God". William's name is below Louisa's towards the bottom of the grave stone.

The grave of Louisa and William Reading in St Andrew's Churchyard, Nuthurst.

Chapter 19

May 1913–April 1922, A Time of War – *signs of major change*

Appendix 3 (The Head Teachers) shows that the retirement of Louisa Reading was followed by a period of temporary Head Teachers, appointed by the West Sussex LEA, before the appointment of Blanche Titterton in December 1913.

During this period there were two serious disagreements between the Managers and the Local Education Authority (LEA) Education Committee.

The first concerned the wish of the Managers to appoint Caroline Millyard as Head Mistress. Caroline was 63 years old and, unsurprisingly, the proposal by the Mannings Heath Managers was rejected by the Education Committee.

The second disagreement concerned some of the terms and conditions of employment that the Mannings Heath School Managers were seeking to impose. The West Sussex County Association of Teachers objected to the Manager's insistence that attendance at the Parish Church on Sundays and Saints' Days should be compulsory on the part of the Head Mistress and Assistant Mistress. The West Sussex Education Committee instructed the Secretary to "interview the Chairman of the Managers". There is no published report of that meeting but it was pointed out that such attendance was not looked upon as legal and was, claimed the Association of Teachers, contrary to the letter and spirit of the Education Act, which was, indeed, correct.

There is no evidence, from subsequent events, that the Managers were able to impose this employment condition although, as a C.E. School, regular attendance at church services was very much part of the school term time syllabus.

It was something of a surprise to find that there were very few mentions of matters concerning the Great War within the Head Teacher's log book. There must have been much concern within the population of the village because at least fifteen households had members serving in the Army between 1914 and

1918. However, this was not really reflected in the life of the school – at least as shown by the Head Teacher's formal records. But maybe the "official record" does not really tell us the whole story.

What references there are in the Log Book are: -

- June 15th, 1915 – The Head Teacher, Barbara Titterton, recorded that "I am giving the children a few minutes conversation on the War every morning, a few notes and am encouraging to ask one another questions as to their opinion about it." This provided an opportunity for sharing issues and drawing on mutual support.
- March 26th, 1917 – Marion Wood, who had replaced Barbara Titterton as Head Teacher, recorded that "The War Savings Association has 16 scholars, who are members. It started a fortnight ago."

In January 1916, a government committee made recommendations concerning the formation of a network of locally based "War Savings Associations". Their objectives were to help to finance the war effort and also the longer-term post-war rebuilding and economic development. Their target was the people able to contribute small amounts and, within a year, thousands of Associations were in active operation.

Chapter 19: May 1913–April 1922, A Time of War – *signs of major change*

By all accounts, Mannings Heath was one of those.

- March 4th, 1918 – At this time, the school was being headed by a succession of temporary teachers. In March 1918, the Head Teacher was Miss M.A. Hodder. She allowed the older children to visit Home Harm to see a balloon which had descended there and, on return to school, to write a composition on what they had seen. She does not specify the type of balloon. It may have been a barrage balloon gone astray from the London defences or it may have been an observation balloon brought back from France.

Observation Balloon, pictured at Slindon Woods in West Sussex.

- March 11th, 1918 – Miss Hodder records that "This afternoon the older children were allowed to see a battle plane at Plummers Plain." Unfortunately, the type of plane and the actual location are not recorded.
- March 12th, 1918 – The older boys started to dig up their playground for growing potatoes. On March 20th, Mr Hunt of Ingleside provided manure for the school gardens which was spread by the boys.

This was a response to the increasing shortages of basic staple foods and the introduction of rationing in January 1918, and also to the particular shortage of potatoes.

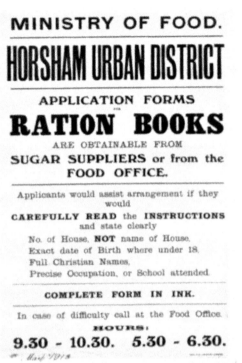 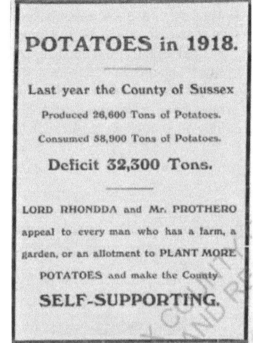

Digging up the playground and the planting of potatoes was a response, by the school, to this public notice concerning the growing gap between the potatoes being produced and consumed.

The potato crop was harvested in mid. September.

May 24th, 1918 – Saw the celebration of Empire Day. Although not specifically a war event, it had been celebrated since 1916 on the anniversary of Queen Victoria's birthday and was used as an opportunity to think about and remember those fighting in the Great War.

The celebration was reported by the Head Teacher, in the Log Book as: -

"'O God our help in ages past', was sung as an opening hymn. Special lessons were taken during the day. At 2.50pm, the Infants joined the Upper Department, and an impromptu concert was indulged in. 'What can I do for England?' and 'Flag of our Country' were sung by the older children. Individual children volunteered to sing and recite, and the proceedings closed with very hearty singing of 'Sussex by the Sea'. The children reverently prayed for the welfare of soldiers, sailors and nurses, and were dismissed at 3.40pm."

November 11th, 1919 – This is the first record of the celebration of Armistice Day. "The wishes of H.M. The King, as expressed in the letter received from the

Chapter 19: May 1913–April 1922, A Time of War – *signs of major change*

Education Authority with regard to the celebration of 'Armistice Day' were duly carried out at 11 o'clock. Attendance good. Half-holiday this afternoon."

On a much lighter note, the war years saw many reports of cricket being played on "The Common" by the pupils. The Log Book entry for 19th June 1916, is a good example. "Being fine, the children had their usual game of cricket on the common on Friday afternoon."

Staying with the theme of the Great War, Appendix 5 contains the results of researching Mannings Heath School pupils who served in the War. Twenty-eight have been identified, from various sources, who joined the school between 1882 and 1904. Three of the twenty-eight are known to have died on active service and one of them, William Glaysher, is recorded as missing at Messines in June 1917. He is remembered on the Glaysher family headstone in the churchyard of St Andrew's Church, Nuthurst.

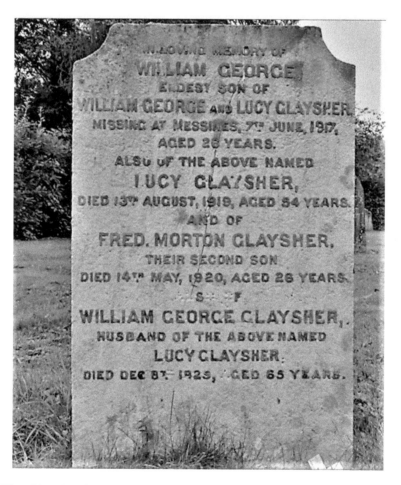

The Glaysher family headstone in St Andrew's Churchyard, Nuthurst.

Messines was a Flanders battle that saw the extensive use of mines in tunnels dug by the Allies under the Messines Ridge occupied by the Germans. In all, twenty-two tunnels were dug and a total of 455 tons of explosives laid, as mines, in the tunnels. The total Allied casualties were some 24,500 with 14,000 being British and 10,500 being from the ANZAC allies. The Germans lost a similar number of men.

Two of those from Mannings Heath School who served are known to have been awarded gallantry medals. Picton Highgate was awarded the Distinguished Conduct Medal and the Military Medal with two bars. Ernest Cowdry was awarded the Military Medal.

In November 1918, Gertrude Ellis became the Head Teacher and the school entered a period of staffing stability after a period of temporary teachers in charge (see Appendix 3).

As well as the celebration of Empire and Armistice Days, as a Church School, attendance at services celebrating Church festivals and Saints days was part of the school term time activities, with services at the "Mission Church" which was just a short walk down Golding Lane and on the other side of Pound Lane (across the cross roads known locally as "Idle Corner"). The services were usually quite short, lasting from 08.45 to 09.30, after which the pupils returned to the school.

Attendance is recorded in the Log Books and, in a typical year, term time services would have been held for: -

- St Paul's Day – January 25th.
- Feast of the Purification – February 2nd
- Ash Wednesday – February 18th
- Feast of St Matthias – February 24th
- Feast of the Annunciation – March 25th
- Service in preparation for Easter – March 31st
- St Philip's and St James's Day – May 1st
- Ascension Day – May 13th
- Feast of St Barnabas – June 11th
- St John the Baptist's Day – June 24th
- Festival of St Peter – June 29th
- St Matthew's Day – September 21st
- St Michael's Day – September 29th

Chapter 19: May 1913–April 1922, A Time of War – *signs of major change*

- St Luke's Day – October 18th
- Feast of St Simon and St Jude – October 28th
- St Andrew's Day – November 30th
- St Thomas's Day – December 21st

We are fortunate in having two personal memories of school life under Gertrude Ellis, from Felix Thorns and Allen Flint, both of whom are recorded in the Memories of Mannings Heath (Ref. 30). Both are worthy of verbatim quotes and provide lovely pen pictures of school life.

Firstly Felix – he was born in December 1909, and was the son of William Thorns of Gagglewood Cottage, the home of the Thorns family for many years. He started at Mannings Heath School in April 1916, and was pupil number 587 in the Register.

His little sketch is: -

"These memoirs would not be complete without reference to the school in those days. With Miss Ellis, 'Granny' to the pupils, as Head Mistress everyone did all of their schooling in one school, from the age of 5 to 14, unless, of course, they won a scholarship and their parents were able to afford to send them to High School. Each classroom *(there were just two classrooms)* had a large coal fire, but even so it was very cold at the back of the classroom in severely cold weather and sometimes your hands were so cold it was difficult to hold a pen and you would ask to warm your hands – until someone slipped a few conkers on the fire which exploded with a loud bang. And that was the end of hand warming for the day.

Once a year on 24th May all the older pupils were taken to Nuthurst School by Bill Seagar from Monks Gate in his Sussex wagon to celebrate Empire Day."

(This is a change from the first celebration in 1919 which took place in Mannings Heath School.)

Now to Allen – he was born in December 1911, and was the son of William Flint. When he started at Mannings Heath School he was just six years old and was living in the forest outside the village. He tells us: -

"The new school was built up the road opposite the Common, and it was there that I started early in 1917. I had to walk from Home Farm, by way of Turf Plain, Sun Oak, Roost Hole and Goldings to the village school. *(This was a trek through Coolhurst to Mannings Heath; quite a hike for a six-year-old.)* When I started school, Mr Reading had retired and a Miss Ellis came as headmistress. *(This was Gertrude Ellis who became Head mistress in November 1918.)* She was a docile old dear, but I know from experience that she could on occasion wield the cane to good effect. *(Gertrude Ellis was, in fact, just 50 years old when Allen started at the school!)*

Poor old girl, she didn't stand a chance with the unruly mob she was expected to teach. She was generally known as 'Granny Ellis'. *(Apart from being in her 50s – no doubt seeming old to the young children – 'Granny' was a natural corruption of her full name which was Gertrude Annie Ellis. It is easy to see where the soubriquet 'Granny Ellis' came from.)*

The slightest attraction, or should I say distraction, saw us boys away. For instance, if the threshing tackle pulled in to Saddlers Farm, we would be up there, getting in everyone's way, and all Granny's calling and hand clapping was of no avail. We would usually get chased away by either the farmer or the engine driver.

If hounds were hunting in the Gaggle Wood *(which was just at the back of the school)* that was fatal, just one blast of the horn, and we would be away, following till the hunt was out of sight, then creeping back to face the consequences.

May 24th was Empire Day, and we had to go down to the Parish Church. The big ones had to walk and the little ones went in a farm wagon. We were usually lectured by some old retired Army officer, who was a school governor, on what he called the 'Empah'."

The Parish Magazine contains, in the edition for February 1922, the very saddest of news. It records the funeral, at St Andrew's Church, Nuthurst, of Miss Augusta Bigg. As the earlier chapters of this history have recorded, throughout her life, Augusta was a staunch, practical and active supporter of Mannings Heath and the school in particular. The Rector recorded in the Parish Magazine that Augusta had been responsible for the building of the Mission Church, the School House and the Presbytery, as well as supporting the building and running of Mannings Heath School. What she would have made of the events recorded in the next chapter, we will never know, but the author cannot but help thinking that the outcome would have saddened her.

The first signs of trouble ahead for Mannings Heath School appeared in April 1922, with the publication of a critical report by Mr Daniell, HMI, acting on behalf

Chapter 19: May 1913–April 1922, A Time of War – *signs of major change*

of the Board of Education (BoE)[66]. The Board is the central Government education authority and, in practice, has primacy over the West Sussex Local Education Authority (LEA) and its Education Committee.

The report, dated 12th April 1922, was the start of what I have described as the "Battle for Mannings Heath School", and is the subject of the next Chapter.

---

66 Nuthurst, Mannings Heath Church of England School Documents in the National Archives. ED21/41261, 62344 and 17544.

Chapter 20

April 1922/November 1924 – the Battle for Mannings Heath School

The report from the HM Inspector of 12th April is key to what followed, and is worth reproducing in full. It says: -

"Instruction.
The work of this small country school has suffered acutely from inadequate staff. Throughout the school year just ended, the Head Teacher has worked in the main room without help of any kind. She has attempted to teach between 30 and 40 children in Standard 2 and upwards – an impossible task. In consequence it has not been possible to give the members of the Junior Section sufficient time and attention to maintain efficiency. It cannot be said that the conditions of Article 10 of the code have been fulfilled, moreover for ten different weeks since 25th November, 1921 the average attendance has exceeded the available teaching power so that there has been an infraction of Article 12(a) of the Code.

In the circumstances, the conscientious work of the Mistress *(Gertrude 'Granny' Ellis)* is worthy of mention. The Infant class is in the charge of a young, inexperienced teacher. She is bright and seems anxious to get on, but would do well to visit, as opportunity offers, a good Infant School so that she may become acquainted with good methods and adjust her standard of work. *(Gertrude Ellis made arrangements for this to take place on 12th July in a large Horsham Infant School).*

It appears that the staff should be strengthened. *(The first draft of the Inspector's report, as contained in Refence 66, contains the additional statement of an alternative which was that 'the attendance at the school should be restricted to children up to Standard 4 and below 11 years of age. Doubtless satisfactory arrangements can be made for the older scholars at some neighbouring school'. This proposal was struck out by the BoE so the Head Teacher and the Mannings Heath School Managers were not aware of it or what it portended for the future. The hand written comments by, presumably, the Inspector's 'boss', also questioned the efficacy of the West Sussex LEA and the Managers in allowing Education Code breaches without remedial action.)*

Padlocks are wanted for both entrance gates so that offices may be protected from public intrusion.

Signed J.B. Daniells, HM Inspector, 29/4/22."

In May, the County Architect visited to commence the planning of school renovations. In view of what follows, this has the "smack'" of right hand not knowing what the left hand was doing within the LEA! The next step was taken by the Managers, no doubt responding to the HMI comments with regard to the adequacy of school staffing. On June 20th 1922, they met (The Rector, Rev. Packenham Gilbert (Chairman), Major F. Bigg, Mr Graves and Rev. EAS Allen). Rev Allen was both the Parish Curate, living at The Presbytery, and the Manager designated as the Correspondent with the Education Authorities. He also took a deep and active interest in Mannings Heath School, taking services, frequently visiting and teaching religious knowledge in the school classes. The purpose of the meeting was to decide on an additional teacher for Mannings Heath and also for Nuthurst where, presumably, similar criticisms had been made.

The Managers received applications from three candidates. The first was a Roman Catholic and was rejected on the grounds of what the Managers described as "local feeling". The second was a man and this was rejected by the LEA. The third was an unqualified teacher who withdrew her application. In the end, on 6th October 1920, a Miss Florence Ellis was appointed as Assistant Mistress.

So, thus far, all the signs to the Managers and the school staff were that the future was looking positive.

There is no record within Ref. 66 but, at some point between June and November 1922, the LEA must have issued advice to the Mannings Heath and Nuthurst School Managers of the Authority's intention to close Mannings Heath School and amalgamate its pupils into Nuthurst School. The letter from the LEA was discussed at the meeting of the Managers at their meeting on 10th November 1922, and the proposal was rejected, but only by the casting vote of the Chairman. There is, in the Ref. 66 documents, a letter from Rev. Edward A. Allen, in his Correspondent role, dated 13th November 1922, to the BoE, as a result of this meeting. He writes: -

"Dear Sir,

The West Sussex Education Committee have asked for the consent of the Managers of the above schools *(Mannings Heath and Nuthurst)* to an amalgamation. They propose to close Mannings Heath School and provide a conveyance to take the younger children to Nuthurst.

Both schools are in one civil and ecclesiastical parish and are both Church schools. Mannings Heath is two miles from Nuthurst and is at one extremity of the parish – Nuthurst schools are in the centre. Mannings Heath School is in the most populous part of the parish, a part of which is slowly growing – the best illustration of the relative positions of the schools will be that every month Mannings Heath gains an attendance holiday – Nuthurst seldom once a year. *(Attendance holidays were half day holidays as a reward for good attendance. The school needed to achieve over 90% of the pupils on the register attending in the month. Rev. Allen was clearly making a favourable case for Mannings Heath on the grounds of keenness of pupils to attend and parents supporting their attendance.)*

The accommodation at Nuthurst is ample for amalgamation. There is an average attendance of children at Mannings Heath of about fifty *(In fact, this is understating the situation because it was nearer 60 than 50 pupils at Mannings Heath School at this time.)* and more children on the register than at Nuthurst. The accommodation at Mannings Heath is for 90 – the buildings are not so convenient as those at Nuthurst – but, of course, on other grounds, closing Nuthurst would be impossible. *(But Rev Allen offers no reasons for this. One must suspect that the reasons are to do with Nuthurst School being a Church School, adjacent to the Parish Church and probably viewed as at the 'ecclesiastical and educational centre' of the Parish.)* The Managers do not wish to put unreasonable obstacles in the way of economy, but we are extremely doubtful if this is a case for such action as closure. *(From other sources, it is clear that there were economic pressures in the post-war period that may have had something to do with the LEA proposals.)*

Instead of settling the matter by a simple vote of the Managers which would have resulted in the rejection of the proposal referred to, the Managers decided to write to the Board *(Note that the letter is to the Government Board of Education in Whitehall and there is no evidence it was copied to the West Sussex LEA. An interesting move on the part of the Managers!)* and ask them to state their attitude towards the scheme.

> I shall therefore be very grateful if you would consider the matter and communicate with me concerning it.
>
> Yours faithfully,
> Edward A.S. Allen – Correspondent"

Edward Allen draws attention, in his letter, to the very good school attendance record in Mannings Heath, as compared with Nuthurst. At the time, Mannings Heath had fifty-one pupils and Nuthurst had fifty-three, so there was no significant difference in school size. It is a significant point to be made in favour of Mannings Heath because improving school attendance was seen as a matter of national importance[67]. Ref. 67 includes information on national average elementary school attendance which shows that, in 1920, the average was 87%. This compares with Mannings Heath where achievement of well above 95% was very usual and, on occasions, 100% was achieved.

The hand written minute response within the BoE documentation is interesting. It reads as though the BoE was not a little peeved because they had not been informed by the West Sussex LEA of their intentions. The first they knew came from Rev Allen's letter on the subject and this placed them, the Board, in a somewhat embarrassing position. In the end, after a number of draft attempts, the BoE replied to both the LEA and the Managers, in a letter dated 24th November 1922, along the lines of: -

- Not being able to express an opinion because they have not received anything from the LEA. However, it is desirable to effect economies where this can be done without prejudice to the educational interests. *(This offers some solace to the Managers and a potential line of argument, if they can exploit it.)*
- Larger schools are more economical than smaller ones and can offer a breadth of educational opportunities that cannot be found in smaller schools. *(This offers a line of solace to the LEA with a potential line of argument they can exploit.)*
- The matter would best be resolved by a "frank discussion" between the Managers and the Local Education Authority. They, the Board, have no doubt their HM Inspector would be "happy to attend, if invited".

This is a masterly piece of Civil Service response worthy of Jim Hacker's Department of Administrative Affairs. It sits the BoE nicely in the not involved category, except through their HM Inspector, but none of the BoE

---

[67] School Attendance 1880-1939. A study of policy and practice.

officials directly involved. However, it offers something to both parties. The other thing not to be forgotten is that it was the Inspector who first proposed a radical change to the status of Mannings Heath School in his unpublished draft report in April. But that fact is only known within BoE and not by the Managers or the West Sussex LEA. One must suspect that the BoE were well aware of that when suggesting that the Inspector attends the "frank discussion". All very devious and Machiavellian, and absolutely worthy of Sir Humphrey.

There is a further little piece of Board deviousness, again in a hand written minute. This is to the effect that, because Mannings Heath School has an average attendance of more than thirty pupils, the Board "rules" do not allow the West Sussex LEA to close it without the agreement of the Managers. But, and it is a big "but", the minute says "…but we need not refer to this point unless asked." One has to suspect that the Managers, in particular, are not aware of this rule and so saw potential closure as a threat against which, in the end, they would have no defence. It would have been nice, but out of character, if the Board had helped them out by telling them. It would have immeasurably strengthened their confidence in being able to keep the school as it was.

The next step along the road was a letter of 27th November 1922, to the Managers and to the BoE, from the West Sussex LEA dated 27th November 1922.

This letter opened unambiguously with the statement that "…The Authority are now proposing to close Mannings Heath School…". It went on to state that the children would be sent either to Nuthurst, or Lower Beeding or to Horsham East Parade. The closure would become effective on 31st March 1923, and that "adequate arrangements should be made for the conveyance of the children… to other neighbouring schools". There is no indication as to who is to make these "adequate arrangements" available. The letter does, however, conclude with "…this proposal of course being subject to the approval of your Board and of the Managers".

There are a number of hand written internal BoE minutes in December 1922, by various civil servants, but the end point is a statement of helplessness from the BoE. "If they *(the Managers)* agree, we *(the BoE)* cannot object; if they *(the Managers)* object, we *(the BoE)* cannot declare the school unnecessary." This is because it has more than thirty pupils.

So, if the Managers had been aware of this, which they were not, and had stuck to their guns, they could have carried the day.

Chapter 20: April 1922/November 1924 – the Battle for Mannings Heath School

However, the BoE was not quite done with the matter because they wrote to the Managers (through Rev. Allen) seeking the views of the Managers on the West Sussex LEA proposal to close the school.

The Managers replied on 16th December 1922, making clear their opposition to closure through a number a number of points: -

- As the basis for closing the school was one of economy, economy which threatens effective education is no true economy.
- It is a matter of simple justice that the school has been provided and maintained for a great many years at a saving in the rates.
- It is rare for Mannings Heath School to fail to achieve an attendance holiday and equally rare for Nuthurst to obtain one.
- The people of Mannings Heath are not "…the slow, bucolic type… and we fear for the efficiency of the education of the children will seriously suffer owing to the hostile co-operation of the parents."
- Some Mannings Heath children attend Horsham schools and go by bicycle. It would be more effective if this practice stopped and they received their education in the school in the district in which they lived.
- The proposal to send children from Mannings Heath by bus is too uncertain because the bus goes to Brighton and expects passengers for the whole trip and is often too full to allow space for young children taking the reactively short trip to school.

There was a quick response dated 22nd December 1922, from the BoE to the West Sussex LEA and the Managers formally stating: -

"I am to remind the Authority that, as the average attendance of this School exceeds 30, it can only be closed with the consent of the Managers and that the Board of Education have no power to declare the School to be unnecessary under Section 19(1) of the Education Act, 1921."

So, at last, the BoE used their authority and gave the Managers the support they needed. Battle won? Well, maybe, but the war was not over. One must suspect that the West Sussex LEA were smarting at having their plans thwarted by the Managers in Mannings Heath who showed no hesitation in communicating, over their head, directly with the BoE.

The next move by the West Sussex LEA took place in October 1923, and it was really a follow up to the unpublished section, which they may have become aware of, in the HM Inspector's report of April 1922, to send the older children from Mannings Heath to other schools. At the time, this proposal seems to have been driven by staff shortages at Mannings Heath.

The West Sussex County Times of 13th October 1923, reported a meeting held in early October between the Managers and representatives of the West Sussex LEA Elementary Education Committee.

The report states that on 4th October, the Sub-Committee *(of the Elementary Education Committee. Just how many committee layers does it take to sort out one little village school? And we think there is too much bureaucracy today!)* "…interviewed by arrangement… a deputation from the Managers of the Nuthurst and Mannings Heath C.E. Schools with reference to the proposal of the Education Committee to send the older children from Mannings Heath to Nuthurst School *(This would more than halve the number of pupils in the Mannings Heath School and, in the longer term, make it non-viable with only about 20 pupils. See Appendix 5.)* … the staff at Mannings Heath being proportionately reduced by one teacher".

The Managers consisted of Rev. C. Pakenham Gilbert (The Chairman and Rector of Nuthurst Parish), Rev. E.A.S. Allen (Correspondent, Nuthurst Parish Curate and long-term supporter of Mannings Heath School), General Ollivant and Major Bigg.

The newspaper report goes on to say, "After discussion, the Deputation *(i.e., the Managers)* fell in with the Committees views. The consequent recommendation was that, from 1st January 1924, all children from Mannings Heath of ten years and over be transferred to Nuthurst School; that on reaching that age children be automatically transferred; that the supplementary teacher now at Mannings Heath School be dispensed with; and an additional, uncertificated *(i.e., lower paid)* teacher be appointed at Nuthurst School to strengthen the staff, the head teacher being in urgent need of assistance."

One can but speculate as to why the Managers acceded to this proposal given their previous opposition to the school closure. Did this, perchance, seem like the lesser evil, or were there less honourable "doings" afoot? Certainly, it does not look like an economical change and, if the Nuthurst School staffing was inadequate for the existing pupils, it did not seem to make educational sense either.

The Whitehall BoE were advised of what became called the "reconstitution" of Mannings Heath School by a hand written internal report from the HM Inspector dated 11th October, following his inspection visit to the school. Although ref. 66 does not contain a typed copy of this report, there clearly was one because the Log Book makes reference to its existence. The report would have been made available to the LEA and to the school Managers.

Chapter 20: April 1922/November 1924 – *the Battle for Mannings Heath School*

A transcript of the HM Inspector's report of 11th October 1924, reads as follows: -

"Since the last Xmas holidays, this school has been reconstituted *(A.W. Currie of BoE uses the word 'decapitated' rather than the euphemistic 'reconstituted' descriptor of the Inspector. See below for the fall out from this report.)* At the end of the term in which they reach 10 years of age, the children attend other schools in the neighbourhood. *(This is, of course, not true. It is what the HM Inspector wanted in his draft report of April 1922, but it is not what the West Sussex LEA intended. Quite specifically, the LEA insisted that all over 10-year-olds would be transferred to Nuthurst – without any option.)* The numbers on the Mannings Heath role have been reduced to 23. *(From the 55 before the 'decapitation'.)* The Assistant Teacher left *(another euphemism; her services were dispensed with by instruction from the LEA as part of the 'plan'.)* at the beginning of the present term so that the Mistress is now single handed. Whilst the top class and half of the second class read well and is responsive to oral questioning on the subject matter, the hand writing is poor and the teaching of arithmetic, both written and mental, leaves much to be desired.

It is very doubtful whether the Mistress *(This is still Gertrude 'Granny' Ellis)*, who latterly has not had much experience with young children, will be able to give the appropriate instruction and necessary grounding to the Infants and Standard 1.

The irregular procedure of supplying one of the older girls to look after the Infants must cease forthwith (Article 11(f)) of the Code and her attendances for the sessions where she has been so employed must be cancelled.

Signed G.R. Theobald, HM Inspector."

It is clear from other minutes in Ref. 66, that the BoE was peeved, to put it mildly. The responsible BoE official (A.W. Currie) wrote to the HM Inspector that: "The LEA has apparently 'decapitated' this school without our knowledge *(this is hinting at a 'stitch up' of some sort because the HM Inspector did know about it and was involved – see later)* or consent. Before raising the point with them we should be glad to know whether you were consulted and whether you consider the arrangements made for the older children [to be] satisfactory. In 1922, the LEA wished to close the school but the Managers objected and as the numbers were over 30 closure was accordingly impossible."

The HM Inspector replied, on 21st October 1924, "Mr Currie. Yes, the LEA consulted me *(It is clear from other documents that the HM Inspector was present at the meeting between the Managers and the LEA Committee on 4th October 1923, so 'consulted' is perhaps understating his involvement. Remember it was the HM Inspector, in his report in April 1922, who first advocated something similar as his 'solution' for Mannings Heath School. It is perhaps no coincidence that this is the way the meeting with the Managers went.) and I consider the arrangements made for the older ones to be satisfactory. But, of course, the LEA should have asked for the BoE's consent. (This must have raised some eyebrows because the HM Inspector is employed by the BoE so, in effect, through him the BoE could be adjudged, by the LEA, if it suited their purposes, which it did, to have given their consent – although Mr Currie may not have been aware of the position until he read this hand written internal minute from his HM Inspector. Sir Humphrey rides again!)"*

The West Sussex Education Committee, one suspects in response to the HM Inspector's reference to the adequacy of the Mistress experience in providing a good grounding to the younger pupils, wrote to the BoE, on 24th October, requesting approval to replace Gertrude Ellis by a young, uncertificated teacher as being able to "take charge of this small School... quite well". (*It is interesting that the West Sussex Education Committee would seek the approval of the BoE to this, relatively minor change, but not for the complete re-organisation [sic – decapitation] of the whole school!)*

At their meeting on 1st December 1924, the Managers rejected the proposal for an uncertificated teacher and rejected the LEA's call for the resignation of Gertrude Ellis following what the LEA described as an unsatisfactory inspection report. They were, in fact, referring to the Report from the HMI on 11th October 1924, which, whilst expressing concern about the Head's experience with younger children, could hardly be described as "unsatisfactory".

The next step by the BoE (Mr Currie) was to send a letter on 27th October 1924, to the LEA. We do not have a typed version of the letter but there is a hand written draft in Ref. 66 that seems to be what was sent. It reads: -

"With reference to the enclosed report *(This is the report from the HM Inspector's visit of 11th October 1924, described above. Although only available as a hand written draft in Ref. 66, it was probably typed and would have been the 'enclosed report'. It is included as a copy in the Log Book entry for November 1924)* upon this school states that the school appears to have been re-organised as a school for younger children only without the approval of the Board. I am accordingly to inquire why the Authority's proposals for the reorganisation of this school were not submitted for the Board's consideration before any steps were taken to give effect to them; and whether the Authority are in a position to

Chapter 20: April 1922/November 1924 – the Battle for Mannings Heath School

furnish a copy of any statement by the Managers of their consent to this reorganisation.

The Board will also be glad to be informed of the exact dates on which the school was reorganised and the names of the schools which the children over 10 years of age are now attending.

Further, I am to request that the Board may be provided with an explanation of the infringement of Article 11(f) of the Code pointed out in the accompanying report and an assurance that the attendances of the pupil in question have been cancelled in respect of the services during which she was irregularly employed in looking after the infants. *(This last is a reference to a girl pupil of 12 years of age who stayed at the school and was 'helping out' in what in earlier days would have been called a monitorial system of education. In this case, it was an expedient to give the Head Teacher some much needed help.)*"

There can be little doubt that Mr Currie of the BoE was, to put it mildly, not best pleased with the turn of events. But, if pressed, he would have to admit that the BoE was to some extent complicit in the outcome because the BoE, via its HM Inspector, had been fully involved in the decision-making process.

The reply from the LEA to Mr Currie's letter, dated 1st November 1924, did not really fully address the concerns he expressed. One would suspect that the LEA were fully aware that they "held all the cards" and that events had moved on so far that back-tracking was not really possible; so, the reply could afford to be fairly anodyne. The response from the West Sussex Education Committee made the following points: -

- The Committee "expressed regret" that the BoE had not been officially informed of the re-organisation proposals but did make the point that the HM Inspector had the matter fully explained to him. This is a not too subtle inference that, in fact, the BoE did know because their Inspector knew. The fact that the Inspector's superior did not know is not a problem for the Education Committee.
- The letter confirms that the HM Inspector was present at the meeting with the Managers.
- After a "full discussion" the following resolutions were passed by the Committee: -
  - "THAT as from January 1st, 1924, all children from Mannings Heath of 10 years of age and over be transferred to Nuthurst C.E. School."
  - "THAT for the future all Mannings Heath children reaching the age of 10 years be automatically transferred to Nuthurst School."

- - "THAT the services of the Supplementary Teacher now at Mannings Heath School shall be dispensed with."
  - "THAT an additional uncertificated Teacher be appointed at Nuthurst C.E. School to strengthen the Staff, the Head Teacher being in urgent need of assistance."
- The Managers, although not in writing, "agreed the foregoing Resolutions and undertook to carry them into effect". *(There is no explanation for why the Managers appeared to accept the Education Committee proposals which, on the face of it, they did not have to do.)*

The next set of internal BoE minutes between Mr Currie and the HM Inspector, G.R. Theobald, were dated between the 4th and 10th November 1924. The first, from Mr Currie, makes the bald statement that "...we can now acquiesce in the decapitation of the School", *(thus the BoE is bowing to the inevitable and accepting that it is too late to undo)* and seeking the views of Mr Theobald on the request for the BoE to approve an uncertificated teacher as Head of the Mannings Heath School.

Mr Theobald's response is interesting on a number of counts: -

- It does not agree that Nuthurst should be the only recipient of pupils from Mannings Heath of over 10 years of age. His understanding appears to be that they should go to Holy Trinity, Lower Beeding, Horsham East Parade or Horsham St Mary's, whichever is most convenient and preferred. *(As he was at the meeting between the Managers and the Education Committee on 4th October, one has to ask how this apparent misunderstanding of what was agreed came about.)*
- He is totally opposed to the employment of an uncertificated Head Teacher for Mannings Heath School, as requested by the Education Committee, in their letter of 24th October, in all the circumstances.

On this second point, he writes to Mr Currie that, "The present Head Teacher *(Gertrude Ellis)* ... will probably be asked to resign and she should be succeeded not merely by a certificated Teacher but indeed a specially selected certificated Teacher experienced in teaching children from 5 to 10 (not an easy job)". He goes on to say, "The LEA *(he means the West Sussex Education Committee)* cannot have it 'all ways'. Before 'decapitation' there were three teachers at Mannings Heath. They got rid of two but added to the staff at Nuthurst. Now they want to substitute for a certificated Teacher a young, uncertificated Teacher who will be single handed *(in a school with two classrooms!)*."

After further minuted debates within the BoE, the BoE writes formally to the West Sussex Education Committee and the Managers on 26th November 1924,

Chapter 20: April 1922/November 1924 – the Battle for Mannings Heath School

with a letter that amounts to the formal end to the Battle of Mannings Heath School.

This final letter states: -

"Sir

With reference to Mr Thompson's *(Thompson is the Secretary of the West Sussex Education Committee)* letters… I am directed to state that the Board have noted that, with the consent of the Managers, this School *(Mannings Heath School)* was re-organised as a school for younger children only as from the 1st January, 1924. I am to request that no children may be retained after the end of the school term in which they reach the age of 10 years, without the previous consent of H.M. Inspector. *(The letter does not say that those over 10 must go to Nuthurst.)*

I am to add that in the existing circumstances, and on this occasion, the Board of Education will not raise objection to the appointment for the present of a suitable uncertificated Teacher as Head Teacher of the School.

It must be understood that the Board reserve the right to review the arrangement and to ask for the appointment of a certificated Teacher if they consider it desirable, and particularly if there is any increase in the number of children in attendance. *(So, the HM Inspector did not get quite all he wanted.)*

I am, Sir,

Your obedient Servant,
F.E. Douglas"

It is difficult to draw conclusions about the events over the previous two and a half years. There was certainly bureaucratic muddle within and between the central government Board of Education and the local West Sussex Education Authority. To what extent this was deliberately manipulative is hard to state. The author suspects that the West Sussex Education Authority was determined, possibly for reasons of making financial savings, in closing or reducing the size of Mannings Heath School, knowing that closing Nuthurst School was not an option. The signs are that they manipulated events to achieve this aim.

To what extent there were other more "political" motives in play is hard to know this far away from the events. It is possible that the direct communication between the Managers and the central government Board of Education may have irritated, and ultimately thwarted, the West Sussex Education Authority in their original intention of closing the school altogether. If so, to what extent the Education Authority manipulated events to win their "second best" of reducing the size of Mannings Heath School is not clear. But one can speculate!

There are a number of references from the Board in needing the agreement of the Managers but the Managers did not seem to realise that they had it in their power to resist the proposals of the Education Authority and, possibly, carry the day.

So, why did the Managers give way, without, it would seem, some serious opposition?

The real supporter of Mannings Heath School was the Curate, Edward Allen. The Log Book shows that the school was very seldom visited by the Rector, C. Pakenham Gilbert or by the other Managers. It may well be that Edward Allen found himself completely "out gunned" by a combination of the other Managers, more interested in preserving and developing Nuthurst School, the Education Committee, without whose support the effective operation of Mannings Heath School was not possible and, last but by no means least, the HM Inspectorate which had come up with the original idea of decapitating Mannings Heath School earlier in 1922.

The end result of this two and a half year "assault" on Mannings Heath School was to: -

- Reduce it from about sixty pupils to about twenty-five pupils.
- Cut it from three teachers educating pupils from 5 to 13 years of age to a single teacher for 5- to 10-year-old infants.

By reducing the numbers, the school became vulnerable to closure altogether, without the need for Managers to agree this action, and for the teaching by uncertificated teachers to be acceptable.

In retrospect, all this effort, upset, politicking…. was completely unnecessary. In 1926, Sir William Hadow, the leading educational reformer of the age, issued his report, known as the Hadow Report, for the Government. It was on the education of the adolescent and made the key recommendation that the split between primary and secondary education should be at age 11.

Within a few years, this had been adopted nationally and the norm was for pupils to go from their Elementary School to a Senior School at age 11. This is

Chapter 20: April 1922/November 1924 – *the Battle for Mannings Heath School*

evident within the Log Books with girls leaving Mannings Heath School at age 11 to go to Oxford Girls Senior School, in Horsham which, today, is the Millais Girls school. And, of course, this age limit of 11 for elementary education applied equally to Nuthurst School and Mannings Heath School.

Within a few years of the "battle" ending, the leaving age from both schools was the same due to changes in the Nation's school age structure.

So, a little more patience and foresight by the authorities could have avoided all the upset and aggravation by the West Sussex Education Committee chasing what turned out to be a very short-term economic gain. However, it must be said that the total number of children in the Parish was falling and it had probably reached a point where two schools was unsustainable in the longer term; so, it was a question of when rather than if.

In the Parish Magazine (Ref 65), the Rector, Rev Pakenham Gilbert, recorded the outcome of the battle thus: -

"A change has been arranged in our Church Schools. The elder children at Mannings Heath are to come to Nuthurst, and now there will be one teacher fewer at Mannings Heath and one more at Nuthurst. It seems that something of this nature had to be done, and we hope the parents will see their way to cooperate for the good of the children. We earnestly hope and pray that the new scheme will work well. The parents can be a great help in this matter."

This is the only report in the Parish Magazine on the matter; there had been no intimation as to what was happening before this formal advice to the Parish, from the Chairman of the Managers, of the outcome.

Chapter 21

December 1923/January 1926 – *the Aftermath of the Battle*

Although Chapter 20 covers the period up to November 1924, and thus overlaps a little with this chapter, that was simply to ensure that all matters concerning the battle were dealt with without introducing other topics. In fact, the impact of the actions by the LEA in reducing the maximum age of Mannings Heath pupils to 10 began to be felt in December 1923, with the first records of pupils leaving Mannings Heath School as a result of the "decapitation".

The Register records (Ref. 1) show that the following pupils left Mannings Heath School in December 1923 and January 1924, as an immediate consequence of the reduced age limit.

Name	Register No.	Age	Date Left
Kathleen Morley	561	15	07/01/1924
Marjorie Ward	562	15	07/01/1924
Percy Mawby	563	14	07/01/1924
Frederick Barden	564	14	31/12/1923
May Still	566	14	07/01/1924
Willie Morley	572	15	07/01/1924
Bertie Morley	575	14	31/12/1923
William Dawes	579	13	31/12/1923
May Garland	585	14	31/12/1923
Dorothy Still	586	14	31/12/1923
Elsie Baldwin	591	14	31/12/1923
George Dawes	612	11	07/01/1924
Elsie Holland	613	11	07/01/1924

Chapter 21: December 1923/January 1926 – *the Aftermath of the Battle*

Name	Register No.	Age	Date Left
Eric Jenner	618	11	07/01/1924
Edith Barden	626	11	07/01/1924
Elsie Gardner	627	11	07/01/1924
Reginald Gardner	605	12	07/01/1924
Rosie Parsons	628	11	07/01/1924
Ernest Still	629	11	07/01/1924
Nora Butcher	630	13	07/01/1924
Kathleen Baldwin	631	11	07/01/1924
Dorothy Tarrant	632	11	07/01/1924
Edith Thorns	648	12	07/01/1924
Gladys Stephens	650	13	07/01/1924
Elsie Burrows	657	15	07/01/1924
Margaret Burrows	658	12	07/01/1924
Gladys Richardson	664	13	07/01/1924
Margaret Richardson	666	12	07/01/1924
Doris Jenkins	672	10	07/01/1924
Kate Jenkins	673	14	07/01/1924
Emily Kempsall	685	12	07/01/1924
Alfred Kempsall*	684	8	07/01/1924
Elsie Kempsall	686	13	07/01/1924

*Alfred Kempsall did not have to leave Mannings Heath School because of the 10-year age limit. He probably left to remain at the same school as his siblings Elsie and Emily.

So, the LEA ruling agreed with the Managers, as described in Chapter 20, made a drastic reduction of thirty-three in the Mannings Heath School registered pupils. This is shown clearly in Appendix 5 – Pupil Numbers – and must have begun the process of making the school a non-viable institution in the longer term. The reduction did, of course, have the benefit of enhancing the longer-term prospects for Nuthurst School by increasing its number of pupils on that register.

It is easy to detect the feelings of frustration from the Head's entries in the log book at the end of the December 1923 term. For all practical purposes the matter had been concluded but, nevertheless, the Head wrote: -

"School closed at 12 o'clock for the Christmas Holidays. No information at present as to re-organisation of the school."

During the Christmas Holidays, pupils must have been advised because the Register shows the leavers as listed above. On January 7th, the Head wrote: -

"School re-opened after the holidays. Under the re-organisation scheme, we are directed to exclude all children over 10. This leaves very small numbers on the register."

On 14th January 1924, the Attendance Officer came to the school for the names and addresses of the children who have had to leave under the new scheme.

Another loss of support for Mannings Heath School occurred in February 1924, when the Curate, Rev Allan, left the Presbytery and Nuthurst to take on a city parish. As we have seen in earlier chapters, he had been a practical and enthusiastic supporter of the school. He was, according to ref 65, given a "send off" party in the Mannings Heath Church Hall.

The second major aftermath concerned the Head, Gertrude Ellis, who had been Head since November 1918.

On 10th October 1924, the HM Inspector, G.R. Theobald *(he who had been "consulted" by the West Sussex Education Committee)*, visited the school. A copy of his report was included in the Log Book by the Correspondent, Rev I.T. Whittle, who had replaced Rev Edward Allen. It must have made very uncomfortable reading for Gertrude Ellis because one of the inspection observations was: -

"... but, in regard to the future of the school it is very doubtful whether the Mistress *(Gertrude Ellis)*, who latterly has not had much experience with young children, will be able to give the appropriate instruction and necessary grounding to the Infants and Standard 1."

In Ref. 66 there is a hand written minute from Mr Theobald to Mr Currie within the BoE in which he hints strongly that Gertrude Ellis will be asked to leave as a follow on from the re-organisation. Matters were clearly coming to a head early in 1925 when the Head wrote in the Log Book for 2nd February that, "The Rev I T

Chapter 21: December 1923/January 1926 – *the Aftermath of the Battle*

Whittle *(presumably the new Curate and Correspondent)* came this afternoon bringing three candidates for the vacant post here shortly".

On 31st March 1925, Gertrude Ellis wrote a final, simple entry in the Log Book as: "I weigh charge of the School to-day". This brief statement brought to an end seven years of her Headship and, latterly, a tumultuous two years that changed the school for ever.

Gertrude was succeeded by Amy Unwins as the new Head of the, now, very small School. Amy was a relatively local lady, having been born in Guildford, the daughter of a nurseryman in Merrow.

There was a small increase in pupil numbers in this first year under the new rules: -

Hilda Richardson and Harry Richardson joined in January from Nuthurst School. They lived at Mill Farm, Coolhurst, so Mannings Heath was an easier school to reach than Nuthurst.

Eileen Tarrant. Had left Mannings Heath in 1924 but re-joined the school in April but left in October.

Cyril Ford. Also came from Mill Farm. Mannings Heath was his first school.

Kathleen Parsons. Started school in June and lived in Winterpick Lane.

John O'Donnell. Living with his grandmother, Mrs Brister, in Church Road. His father was an engineer, working in Canada.

Alice and James Gander. Living in Crofton Cottages, having come to Mannings Heath from Wiltshire. Joined the school in November.

The remainder of 1925 proceeded in a fairly orderly fashion with few real highlights. There were, however, one or two incidents of note, although the change in numbers and the change in the age rules does not seem to have had any further repercussions.

- Rev IT Whittle, as Curate and Correspondent, replaced by Rev Herbert MS Collier, also took on the regular Religious Knowledge teaching.
- The school continued with its very good attendance record and continued to have the regular attendance holiday rewards.
- The HMI, GR Theobald, paid a visit in July. No formal report but he did call attention to smells from the boys and the girls cloak rooms, and litter in the cloak rooms.

- In November, the school was closed for two weeks because of an outbreak of scarlet fever in Mannings Heath. Even after the school re-opened, scarlet fever was reducing attendance right into December.
- The first full inspection took place on 1st December and was carried out by Rev G Standish, Assistant Diocesan Inspector.

The Inspection Report was generally favourable and supported the work of Amy Unwins which, in the circumstances, says much for her abilities. However, the report did draw the attention of the Managers to the need to provide pictures and books to support the Religious Knowledge teaching.

Chapter 22

January 1926/January 1939 – *a period of stability in the life of Mannings Heath School*

1926 was a quiet year of normality and was, one suspects, most welcome as such.

The pupils continued the practice of attending services at the Mission Church throughout the year. The services meant that teaching started at 09.45 after a 45-minute service. This year, services for the pupils were held to celebrate the Conversion of St Paul, the Purification of the Virgin Mary, Ash Wednesday, the Annunciation of the Blessed Virgin, Ascension Day and St John the Baptist Day.

On 12th March, school finished early and the school did not open on the 13th. This was to allow the children to attend the British Empire Shopping Week Exhibition. The British Empire Shopping Week was part of a government initiative to strengthen trade, social and scientific links between the nations of the Empire.

One of the many posters promoting trade between the nations of the Empire and published in 1926.

There were twelve admissions in the year and eight leavers, so giving a net gain.

The admissions were: -

Denys Eyles. Living at Swallowfield Farm. The family had come from Hitchen.
Lionel Coleman. Living in Church Road having moved from Highbury Park.
Sybil Eyles. Younger sister of Denys.
Ivy Jestico. Living at Rose Cottage and coming from Bookham in Surrey.
Celia Ford. From Mill Farm, Coolhurst.
Ruby Stevens.
Thomas Richardson. Living at The Cabin in Monks Gate and was at East Parade, Horsham.
Alfred Kempshall. Living at Sadlers Farm and coming from Sittingbourne.
Leonard Lewis. From the Golf Club.
Queenie Lewis. Leonard's older sister.
Marjorie Weedon. Living at White Cottage and from London.
Leonard Hole. Living at The Goldings having moved from Bolney.

In March 1927, the school was given its first full inspection, post decapitation and settling down to the new age rules, by G.R. Theobald. His report is worth including, in full, because of the central role that he played in the events resulting in the "decapitation".

His report records that Mannings Heath School is categorised as a Junior Mixed School and has E42/98/5 as its registration number. His report reads: -

"Since the report of 1924 was written a new teacher has taken charge who was formerly engaged in teaching Infants in a neighbouring school. She has adapted herself skilfully to her new role, and is successful in her instruction of her pupils, who range in age from 5 to 10 years. A pleasant and industrious spirit prevails: the teaching is bright, and the children who are expected to remain here 2 years and more are very promising.

Of those few *(in fact there were 7 who left for other schools after the HMI visit)* who next month will be passing on to other schools, the reading is satisfactory and the penmanship fairly good; but knowledge of arithmetic is backward.

As reported to the Local Education Authority under Circular 1143, the desks in the school are very unsatisfactory."

Chapter 22: January 1926/January 1939 – *a period of stability*

This report, along with the report from the Diocesan Inspector, confirms that Amy Unwins was, indeed, a first-class teacher and Mannings Heath was lucky to have her.

The next three years, up to 1930, passed calmly with little excitement. The normal routines continued: -

- Diocesan Inspections that continued to praise the work of the Head.
- Weekly visits by the LEA Attendance Officer to check on absentees and the Register. The school continued with a good attendance record and were regularly rewarded by a half day holiday granted by the Managers.
- Numbers on the Register remained at about twenty pupils.
- The usual outbreaks of illnesses, including an influenza outbreak in 1928.
- Regular attendance at the Mission Church for early morning services on Saints Days and other Church festivals.
- Regular medical and dental inspections and treatments.
- Weekly Scripture lessons by the Curate, Rev. R.M.S. Collier, until he left the parish in March 1929. He was replaced, but only for a year, by Rev. Huxtable who left in March 1930.
- No further full inspections by the HMI but G. Theobald, HMI, paid several short visits to the school. There were no HMI reports from these informal visits.

In 1929 the Scholastic Souvenir Co came to the school to photograph the pupils. We are fortunate to have a copy from Mrs Jesse Hill (as a pupil, she was Jesse Thorns) with some of the pupils identified by name.

1929 Mannings Heath School Photograph

Back Row (from left to right):
Jim Gander (aged 10, living at Crofton Cottages, No. 700 on pupil register)
Violet Dawes (aged 9, living at Church Cottages, No. 688 on pupil register)
Edwin Boniface (aged 9, No. 728 on pupil register)
Phyllis Ford (aged 8, living at Mill Farm, Coolhurst, No. 705 on pupil register)
Horace Mitchell (aged 10, No. 693 on pupil register)
Maude Wells (aged 8, living at The Links, No. 718 on pupil register)
Leslie Kempshall (aged 9, living at Saddlers Farm, No. 708 on pupil register)
Ernest Philip Peter Wells (aged 10, living at The Links, No. 717 on pupil register)
Amy W Unwins – Head Teacher. See Appendix 3.

Middle Row (from left to right):
Tony Bateman (aged 7, living at The Chestnuts, No. 713 on pupil register)
Leonard Price Lewis (aged 8, living at the Golf Club, No. 709 on pupil register)
Ivy Joan Jestico (aged 7, living at Rose Cottage, No. 704 on pupil register)
Enid Alice Thorns (aged 6, No. 725 on pupil register)
Not identified – see Note below.

Front Row (from left to right):
Enid Charman (aged 11, living at Coneys Cottage, No. 682 on pupil register)
Hilda Charman (twin with Enid. No. 681 on pupil register. Both were granted special permission to remain at Mannings Heath School beyond 10 years of age due to poor health)

Chapter 22: January 1926/January 1939 – *a period of stability*

Cyril Ford (aged 9, living at Mill Farm, No. 696 on pupil register)
Not identified – see Note below.

Not identified – see Note below.
Note – Three boys are not identified; from a review of the pupil register (Ref 52), it is most probable that they are John O'Donnell, Henry Berrett and Alan Bailey.

In December 1929, the Rector, Rev Pakenham Gibson had to retire due to ill health. His successor was to be Rev Rowland D Mertens who was inducted by the Bishop of Chichester in October 1930. Rowland Mertens was born in Lucerne, Switzerland, and gained his theology BA at Kings College, London. After graduating, his first job was that of an Assistant Master teaching in a boys school. We will see that he took a personal and active role in the life of Mannings Heath School both as a teacher of scripture and as the Chairman of the School Managers.

As usual, the appointment of the Rector of Nuthurst was made by the Bishop of London who had the right of patronage for the Parish of Nuthurst. Rev Mertens is listed in the London Diocese Book for 1919 as being a "Surrogate" appointed by the Chancellor of London. He had previously been a Curate in Limehouse and Vicar of Notting Hill and Arlington, so he had been part of the Bishop of London's team for many years before his Nuthurst appointment.

He made his first visit to Mannings Heath School on 17th October 1930, and took morning prayers and taught a scripture lesson.

At the end of the Summer term 1931, Amy Lewin resigned and when the School re-opened, on 2nd September, after the Summer holiday, Elizabeth Olive Lewry (see Appendix 3) commenced duty as the Head Teacher and just two weeks later, the school was given an inspection by Mr H. Allsopp, his report is included in the Log Book and reads: -

"This single teacher school now contains only 21 infants and juniors.

The new Head teacher has made a promising start and has fully realised the needs of the school. She is rightly stressing the importance of securing more accuracy, neatness and thoroughness in the 3 Rs.

At present the juniors seem unable to concentrate their attention or to work steadily and quietly without close supervision. It is therefore recommended that, for a time at any rate, all the children should be taught in one room.

Other points discussed were the quality of the reading matter available, the desirability of developing cursive writing in Standard 3 and the schemes of work in History and Geography."

In the circumstances, the Head and the Managers must have been reasonably satisfied that there were no serious problems raised by the HMI.

Shortly after this inspection, Jessie Thorns was admitted to the school as a pupil. She was pupil number 748 in the register and was admitted on 31st October 1931, when she was just 3 years old. She left on 6th April when she was 11 years old having reached Standard 4, which was very creditable.

Jessie lived at Gagglewood Cottage with her father, Ernest, who was a dairy farmer, mother Rosa, sister Enid and brother David.

We are indebted to Jessie on two counts. Firstly, she was the provider of many of the school photographs in various chapters of this story and, secondly, she has given us some reminiscences of life in the school in the 1930s.

Jessie's story, written in 2016 when she was 88 years old: -

"I used to run away from home *('home' was Gagglewood Cottage)* and go and stand at the school gate so they let me start when I was three years old.

There were two classrooms but only one teacher *(the teacher was Elizabeth Olive Lewry who must have taken pity on the little 'girl at the gate'.).* There was no electricity so, in the winter, we had a hanging oil lamp and coal fires. There was a row of toilets at the bottom of the playground in front of the school *(in fact, the playground and toilets were behind the school, away from Golding Lane.).* Boys and girls had to share, we didn't have flushed toilets; it was a pail with a seat. We had a man come once a week with a horse and cart to empty the pails and take the mess away. One day, my friend was in there when a tramp came out of the wood and opened the door so, after that, we had to go in two's; one stood outside while the other was inside.

The teacher was able to use the cane those days. We didn't have pen and ink but only pencils. We didn't have any toilet rolls so we had to cut up newspaper in squares and hang it up with a bit of string inside the door.

We had an hour for lunch but we couldn't take any food into school so we had to go home to lunch. There were no desks; we had tables and chairs. The teacher had a blackboard and easel which she wrote everything on with white chalk.

I really loved it; it was some of the best days of my life".

Early in 1932, Elizabeth Lewry became suspicious about the quality of the school water supply and, as a result, the Rural District Council Sanitary

Chapter 22: January 1926/January 1939 – *a period of stability*

Surveyor came to the school on 12th May to take a sample for quality analysis. At the end of May, the Surveyor reported that the analysis had shown that the water supply was not fit for drinking purposes and that the School Correspondent, appointed by the Management Committee, Mr C.E. Tuppen, would be informed.

What we do not know is what happened as a result – but perhaps in the light of Jessie's remarks about the sanitary arrangements and the fact that the water supply was from a well, we should not be too surprised.

The Log Book continues to record the regular, usually weekly, scripture lessons from the Rector, Rev. Mertens, and, in fact, on an occasion in October 1932, he took over the role of Head Teacher when Elizabeth Lewry was not well.

Throughout 1932 numbers fluctuated as pupils joined and left, but always in the band between twenty and twenty-five pupils. Attendance continued to be very good and consistently above 95%, except when a bout of sickness was present in the hamlet. This high level of attendance had much to do with the support from the parents for the school. This was specifically mentioned by the Diocesan Inspector in September 1932, when, in his report, he wrote that: -

"Particularly encouraging were the evidences of co-operation and contacts between school and parents."

1932 ended in a celebratory fashion. On 15th December the Managers decided to give to the School an HMV Table Top Gramophone and records. On 20th December the pupils provided an entertainment for parents, friends and the School Managers – and the gramophone was used to entertain them during the interval. The money raised from this entertainment was used to fund a trip to the pantomime in Horsham in January. On 22nd December Mrs Florence Abbey of Sedgwick Park gave a party for the pupils of both Nuthurst and Mannings Heath Schools.

1933 saw the school closed in January because of an influenza and whooping cough outbreak in Mannings Heath. This caused Anthony Bateman to miss out on sitting his Scholarship exam for Collyer's but fortunately he was given a further opportunity at the end of January. He was successful and went to Collyer's after the Easter holiday.

In Jessie Thorns story recounted earlier in this chapter, she recalled an incident of a "tramp" appearing out of the woods behind the school when a friend of hers was using the toilets. Elizabeth Lewry tells us a little more of the incident in the Log Book entry for 3rd May 1933, as follows: -

"I gave permission for Eileen Jestico, a pupil of this school, to visit the Girl's Offices at 10am. She returned a few minutes later in a very perturbed state, saying that, while there, a man had accosted her. I immediately sent for the police and the child's mother with the result that later a man was held in custody."

After that, events moved swiftly because, on 4th May, the school was closed for the morning and Elizabeth Lewry attended the Police Court where the man charged pleaded guilty. She does not tell us what the sentence was but Jessie recounts the safeguarding action taken by the pupils from then on.

Later in the year a school photograph was taken.

1933 Mannings Heath School Photograph

Back Row (from left to right):
Reg Stepney (aged 8, living at The Common, No. 737 on pupil register)
George Gander (aged 6, living at Crofton Cottages, No. 766 on pupil register)
John Brown (aged 7, living at Coolhurst Lodge, No. 749 on pupil register)
Michael Morris (aged 7, living at Little Fosters, No. 758 on pupil register)
Elizabeth Olive Lewry – Head Teacher. See Appendix 3.

Middle Row (from left to right):
Tony Cox (aged 6, living at Church Road, No. 762 on pupil register)
Kathy Barden (aged 5, daughter of Ernest Barden, No. 756 on pupil register)
Barbara Morris (aged 8, living at Little Fosters, No. 759 on pupil register)
Wendy Eyles (aged 7, living at Swallowfield, No. 751 on pupil register)
Enid Thorns (aged 7, living at Gaggelwood Cottage, No. 725 on pupil register)
Eileen Jestico (aged 7, living at Dunhorse Cottage, No. 744 on pupil register)

John Tomlinson (aged 7, living at Rose Cottage, No. 730 on pupil register)
Peter Ford (aged 7, living at Mill Cottages, No. 740 on pupil register)

Front Row (from left to right):
Alfred Ansell (aged 5, living at The Common, No. 755 on pupil register)
Robin Morris (aged 6, living at Little Fosters, No. 760 on pupil register)
Dorothy Gatland (aged 4, living at 2 North Cottages, No. 768 on pupil register)
Jessie Thorns (aged 5, living at Gagglewood Cottage, No. 748 on pupil register)
Peter Morris (aged 5, living at Little Fosters, No. 764 on pupil register)
Joyce Ford (aged 5, living at Mill Cottages, No. 770 on pupil register)
Enid Simpson (aged 6, living at North Lands, No. 753 on pupil register)

The various Inspector's reports on the school during Elizabeth Lewry's time as Head show her qualities, which resulted in her applying for the position of Head of a Littlehampton Council Elementary School.

On 13th October Elizabeth Lewry's Log Book entry reads: -

"I informed him *(the Rector, Rev Mertens)* that the West Sussex Education Committee... had appointed me to the Headship of Littlehampton East Street C Infants School."

To prepare for taking up this position, the West Sussex Education Committee gave her leave of absence for a week of observation at a London County Council School to prepare for her new and larger role, which she was due to take up in January 1934. The Log Book contains her simple statement of resignation effective from 31st December 1933.

Her new school was built in 1878, just five years before Mannings Heath School and still survives, in East Street, but as a Youth Centre.

Elizabeth Lewry's Littlehampton School where she became Headmistress in January, 1934.

When the School re-opened after the Christmas holiday on 8th January 1934, the position of Headmistress was taken by Muriel Amy Howard, initially on a supply teacher basis, as recorded in the Manager's Minute Book. She became the appointed Head in March 1935.

Muriel Howard – Head Teacher from January 1934.
She lived at Frederick House, Monks Gate whilst at Mannings Heath School.

Over the next five years the Log Book shows that school life carried on without any major upsets.

- The Rector, Rev Mertens continued to give weekly scripture lessons as well as acting as the official Correspondent for dealings with the West Sussex Education Committee and Chairman of the Management Committee for both Nuthurst and Mannings Heath Schools.
- There were annual inspections by the Diocesan Inspector and regular visits from the LEA's Inspectors.
- There were matters of discipline when behaviour got out of hand but nothing too untoward.
- The school had its weekly visits from the LEA Attendance Officer checking on absentees. This was never a serious issue at this school where attendances were regularly recorded as over 95% of those on the register.
- There were regular medical inspections of the pupils by the schools Medical Officer, both to identify any problems and to follow up on progress where treatment was taking place.

Chapter 22: January 1926/January 1939 – *a period of stability*

- Pupil numbers on the register continued to be between twenty and twenty-five, and the pupil age range was from 5 to 11.
- Each January, pupils approaching 11 years of age sat the Preliminary Qualifying Examinations for Special Places in Horsham Secondary Schools. This was for entry to the Oxford Road Senior School or, for the brightest, Collyers in Hurst Road. For example, in 1933 Anthony Bateman succeeded in winning a place at Collyers and, in 1935, Derek Cox and John Tomlinson joined the Oxford Road Senior School which, at that time, had about 150 boys and 140 girls as pupils.

Perhaps the best way to get a picture of life at the school is to produce an edited Head Teacher's Log Book extract from a school year – say 1937 – as an example.

11th Jan. School re-opened this morning. Reg Stephney 11yrs has been transferred to Oxford Road Senior Boys School.

12th Jan. School Nurse visited at 11.15. Head Inspection held.

13th Jan. 1 ton coal received from Hall & Co.

18th Jan. Roof drain pipe blocked near lobby. Water splashes into lobby. This will be reported to the Managers this evening.

19th Jan. When leading in from play at 2.45p.m. George King slipped and fell, cutting his head on an infant's table. There was a bruise on his left temple. Accident reported to Clerk of County Council.

20th Jan. Mr Randall, School Manager and builder cleared the blocked drain.

26th Jan. Preliminary Qualifying Examinations for Special Places in Secondary Schools was held in school this morning. One of the seven children taking the exam was absent.

29th Jan. 15 children absent owing to snow and colds.

8th Feb. Preliminary Qualifying Examination for Special Places in Secondary Schools was held this morning for Peter Ford who was absent on Jan 26th, the original date of the exams.

11th Feb. At playtime, Edna Thompson said that her lunch – a chocolate biscuit – was missing from her coat pocket. A thorough search of all children's outdoor clothes and the desks was made. The lunch was not found. In future, all lunches and dinner bags are to be given into teachers charge when children arrive at school. This is the third occasion recently on which lunches have been missed.

12th Feb. Miss Moodie (HMI) paid school a short visit at 3.15pm. Douglas Sheppard, aged 5 years, admitted taking and eating the lunch lost yesterday. Teacher spoke to the child alone and not in front of the other children.

15th Feb. Jessie Thorns has chicken pox.

26th Feb. Received two new dual locker desks.

15th Mar. The school will be closed all day tomorrow with Managers' permission. There is to be a meet of foxhounds on the Common outside school and this would make it difficult to hold school as usual.

25th Mar. School closed after the morning session for the Easter Holliday.

5th Apr. School opened this morning.

12th Apr. School closed this afternoon until 16th Apr. in order that Head teacher may attend Physical Training Course.

21st Apr. (Pupil A), who was put in the spare room for disobedience, made several large scratches on the door.

26th April (Pupil B) was put in the spare lobby for 10 mins this morning and for an hour this afternoon as he lost his temper. He made some marks on the lobby door.

27th Apr. (Pupil B) was put in the spare lobby this morning for 10 mins for disobedience.

6th May. School closed all day for Ascension Day. Head Teacher took four of the older children to a service at Nuthurst Church. (This is something of a contrast with earlier times when the whole school regularly attended services at the Mission Church in Mannings Heath.)

11th May. School closed after the noon session until Wednesday, 19th May, for Coronation (of George VI) and Whitsun Holidays.

8th Jun. Received PT apparatus from Messrs. Linkins.

10th Jun. Fred Woolven and Alfred Ansell, two children who attend schools in Horsham and were on holiday today, created a nuisance during the afternoon by throwing mud and stones into the lobby. Daphne Topper fell over by the old desk in the yard.

15th Jun. At play 10.50 a.m. Daphne Topper fell over by the old desk in the yard and came in complaining she had hurt her left shoulder. Head Teacher, who was afraid her collar bone was injured, sent Eileen Jestico home to the child's mother with a note. At 11.35, Mrs Topper called and took Daphne and Peter Topper home.

Chapter 22: January 1926/January 1939 – a period of stability

16th Jun. Daphne Topper has a greenstick fracture of the left collar bone.

24th Jun. Miss Moodie, HMI, visited the school from 10.20 a.m. until 12 noon. School closed for the afternoon in order that the Head Teacher could take four children to the Sports in Horsham.

29th. Jun. Miss Moodie HMI visited the school from 9.45 a.m. till 12 noon. (This was for the purpose of carrying out a full school inspection.)

30th Jul. School closed at 3.45 p.m. for Summer Holidays. Peter Ford, John Brown and Phyllis Sheppard have left for Senior School at Oxford Road, Horsham.

6th Sept. School re-opened this morning. George King has whooping cough. SMO and MOH notified.

14th Sept. The Caretaker reported that the drinking water from the school house was cloudy this morning. Children were advised not to drink it.

17th Sept. I have received the report from HMI as follows. (This is the report of the HMI inspection visit on 29th June.)

"Inspected on 29th June 1937
Report by HMI Miss A.M. Moodie

This is a small school consisting of one class with, at the time of Inspection, 24 names on roll. It is housed in a building possessing no modern amenities. The ages of the children range from just under 5 years to 11 years giving roughly an average of four children in each age group. An added difficulty is presented by a certain instability in the population, for example, nine of the 24 children have been admitted during the present school year. The mistress has, therefore, no easy task and she took charge of the school with little previous experience. She has organised the formal work carefully. Reading is well taught and all the children of an age to do so can read. In arithmetic, the children's attainments are relatively less good than in English.

The Physical Training lesson seen was taken on the right lines but under difficult conditions for the playground is small and its surface uneven.

The tone of the school is pleasant. The children are given small responsibilities through which they may learn habits of independence. What they lack is the opportunity for activities such as Music, Nature Study and Handwork which are difficult to organise with a group of children of such varying ages."

6th Oct. Yesterday afternoon and this afternoon, (Pupil C) was very insolent and disobedient. She refused to go into the spare room and had to be pushed in. The door handle had to be tied to keep her there.

12th Oct. Miss Croucher, Physical Training Organiser for West Sussex visited the school.

14th Oct. (Pupil C) again was thoroughly insolent and disobedient. She was slapped several times on the hand and once on the leg for kicking the floor. She was disobedient and insolent again later and, when struggling with the teacher, scratched her own hand.

18th Oct. The school Medical Officer held a clinic for inoculation against diphtheria.

21st Oct. Mr Wood, representing the Scholastic Souvenir Co. called this morning, after previously notifying the Head Teacher, to take the children's photographs.

28th Oct. (Pupil C) was extremely rude and insolent and hit other children with books and spit. She had to be put into the spare room for 10 minutes as a punishment.

29th Oct. Received cleaning materials from Messrs Piggott, Horsham. All correct.

1st Nov. During the weekend, a tile has come off the roof and there is a leak in the ceiling of the spare room. The Post Master told the Head Teacher that it is necessary to have a letter box at the school. The Managers will be informed.

3rd Nov. Head Teacher mentioned to (mother of Pupil C) that her daughter was being very troublesome at school.

4th Nov. Mr Randall, School Manager, measured the yard with a view to it being re-surfaced.

11th Nov. Two minutes silence observed at 11.00 a.m. A lady came to school at 10.20 a.m. to sell poppies.

22nd Nov. The clinic for the second set of inoculations against diphtheria was held at the school. Other children from Mannings Heath, but not yet of school age were also inoculated.

26th Nov. 7 out of 23 pupils absent due to an epidemic of whooping cough. (This epidemic lasted until mid-December with, on average, 7 pupils absent throughout the period.)

29th Nov. One of the planks in the floor of the spare room is rotten and has broken. The Managers will be informed.

8th Dec. When the children entered school this morning, they were, as usual, given exercises in the classroom to warm them. They were standing in the clear

Chapter 22: January 1926/January 1939 – a period of stability

spaces in the room. George King, when doing trunk downward drop, struck his head on the back of an infant's chair. He made a deep cut over his left eye. The Head Teacher sent the other children into the yard and took George King home – about 2 mins. walk, and returned after an absence of about 5 mins. Accident will be reported to the Clerk of the County Council.

9th Dec. Children assembled for the Diocesan Inspection of Religious Instruction.

17th Dec. June Sumner attended Lower Beeding School for inoculation against diphtheria. Two children still absent with whooping cough.

21st Dec. The Correspondent (Rector, Rev. R.D. Mertens) *brought the report of Inspection of Religious Instruction* (Inspection carried out on 9th Dec.). *It read:* -

>"Diocese of Chichester
>Rural Deanery of Horsham
>Report of Religious Instruction
>Mannings Heath School
>Mixed Department
>Inspected by Rev. H.E. Stewart (with Rev Mertens present)
>on 9th December, 1937.

The Teacher in this school has a difficult task in arranging the lessons to suit the varying ages of the children.

She very wisely separates the children into two groups and the results are clear evidence of the ability and care she is putting into the teaching.

The elder children answered well and showed a very good knowledge of the ground covered in recent lessons.

The expression work of the younger ones showed freedom and, in general, the school more than justifies its existence.

The Inspector appreciated his talk with Miss Howard and her readiness to do the best that is possible in this school.

>Signed
>H.E. Stewart"

21st Dec. The school will open this afternoon at 1.15 p.m. and close at 3.30 p.m. in order that the children may be ready for the bus which will take them to a treat given by Mrs Abbey (of Sedgwick Park) at Nuthurst School. (Pupil B) has been insolent and rude today in the extreme. He scratched Jean Thompson on the head and tore up his sum book.

23rd Dec. The School closed after the noon session for the Christmas Holidays. It will re-open on Monday 10th January 1938.

Authors Note – The huge sigh of relief at the end of this term can almost be felt off the written page of Muriel's Log Book!

The Log Book record for 1938 showed much the same pattern of events as 1937: -

- Numbers of pupils remained at between twenty and twenty-five.
- The Rector continued to support the scripture teaching as well as acting as the Correspondent.
- The same three children, identified earlier as pupils A, B and C to protect their anonymity, continued to cause trouble throughout the year.
- There continued to be a flow of minor injuries to pupils – both self-inflicted accidents and as a result of the actions of pupils A, B and C.
- Sicknesses and weather continued to be the only cause of reductions in the attendance record.
- Repairs to the school building continued to be needed through the year. All were minor items such as blocked drains, a broken floor board, cracked window glass, leaking gutter, but indicative of a building showing its age and condition.

There were, however, some particular events in 1938 that broke new ground. The first was that on 25th February, the Head Teacher was given leave to close the school for two days so that she could attend a National Union of Teachers Refresher Course in Worthing.

Although the Union had been in existence since 1873, this is the first mention of any Mannings Heath teacher being a member or attending any Union event. In the 1930s, the NUT reached over 150,000 members, most of whom were in the Primary sector. In particular, they supported the 1926 Haddow report which led to the primary/secondary boundary being set at 11 years of age. Looking back to Chapter 20 and the battle for Mannings Heath School, had the West Sussex LEA been a little more patient and the Haddow report conclusions foreseen, it would have rendered the battle and subsequent "decapitation" of Mannings Heath School a totally unnecessary step for no long-term benefit.

At the end of March, the School had a visit from Mr P.J. Moss who was the Assistant Commissioner for the National Savings Committee. This visit took place before the Annual Meeting of the West Sussex National Savings movement reported in the Bognor Regis Observer of 6th July. The report showed clearly that that the movement was declining in membership and it is likely that the visit from Mr Moss was part of the drive to reverse this trend.

National Savings Movement poster of the late 1930s

It is quite likely that he would have brought posters like this to leave at the school to encourage joining the movement.

It was at the Annual Meeting in July that Mr Moss was promoted to the position of Assistant Commissioner.

On 5th April, the school was visited by Miss Gardener who was a Lecturer in Education at Leeds College and a friend of Muriel Howard. She was there for the whole afternoon.

Muriel Howard was clearly concerned to create a good relationship with the Oxford Road Girls School to which girls from Mannings Heath were transferred at 11 years of age. So, she invited the Oxford Road School Head to spend an afternoon at Mannings Heath School. Miss Wilson, the Oxford Road Head spent the afternoon of 24th May at Mannings Heath School. On that day, the school was also visited by County Council representatives to inspect the building prior to its internal decoration. Muriel took the opportunity to ask for a new grate to be fitted in the main room, which was done.

In November, the school was closed for two days to allow the Head Teacher to attend a conference on Religious Education organised by the LEA and held in Chichester. Interestingly, this conference was hosted by the LEA and not the Diocesan authority dealing with the C of E Schools in West Sussex.

On 17th November, Muriel was visited, at her School, by her parents and her sister.

The school closed on 21st December for the Christmas holiday and re-opened on 9th January 1939. 21st December forms an appropriate end date for this chapter for, in 1939, everything changes for the war years.

Before we leave for the war years, we are fortunate that Muriel Howard was, among her other interests, a keen photographer. In May,1938, she took a number of photographs of life at the school and I am indebted to Andrew Howard for some of the results.

This shows pupils at play behind the school.
The toilets can be seen on the right.

Chapter 22: January 1926/January 1939 – *a period of stability*

This picture is taken on the left-hand side of the school, looking from Golding Lane. It shows, from left to right, Daphne Topper, Peter Topper, Jessie Thorns and Eileen Jestico. Very faintly, there is an image of someone, unnamed, peering from the doorway of the school building on the left of the picture.

From left to right, we have two Thompson sisters with Kathy Ansell and Peter Daniels. The photograph was, again, taken on the left-hand side of the school.

This one is, again, taken on the left-hand side of the school building. Unfortunately, the children are not named but the toilets are clearly visible on the left of the picture. The picture also shows the school bell above the left-hand window. This bell is now in the Horsham Museum.

Chapter 23

1939/1945 – *the war years*

Up until the end of August in 1939, the Log Book entries by the Head Teacher give no hint of the impending war time upheavals to come. The school went through its normal routines: -

- Weekly visits by the Attendance Officer.
- Scripture lessons and Register checking by the Rector.
- Pupils being entered for the examinations for Horsham senior schools.
- Inspection by the Diocesan Inspector with the usual complimentary remarks on the quality of the Head Teacher's work with her pupils.
- Children misbehaving and the usual crop minor accidental injuries.
- Maintenance and repairs to the fabric of the school.

In fact, throughout the six years of World War 2, the Head Teacher's Log Book tells us little of the impact of some major local war incidents on the work of the school and the pupils, and life in the village.

Returning now to school life, on 23rd March, the routine of school photographs continued with the pupils being photographed by the Scholastic Souvenir Co.

1939 Mannings Heath School Photograph

This photograph shows twenty-four pupils, which is all those on the Register in March 1939.

Back Row (from left to right):
Muriel Howard – Head Teacher, John Sumner, Ruth Dale, George Gander.

Second Row from the back (from left to right):
Andrew Ford, Eileen Sheppard, Douglas Sheppard, Robert Dale, Pat Brown, Daphne Topper, Jessie Thorns, June Sumner, Joyce Ford, George Still.

Third Row from the back (from left to right):
Don Bateman, Rosemary Sheppard, Peter Topper, Edna Thompson, Kathy Ansell, Joy Godsmark, Peter Daniels, Jean Thompson.

Front Row (from left to right):
George King, Dorothy Thompson, Austen Mangles.

The first hint of what was to come is the Log Book entry, by the Head Teacher, for 28th August 1939, in the school summer holiday, which reads: -

"Head Teacher was on duty today to help with reception of evacuated children if necessary. At 3.45 p.m. members of the local evacuation committee rearranged the school rooms."

Chapter 23: 1939/1945 – *the war years*

This is the first mention of the local planning that was being done but, of course, evacuation planning had been going on for some time before this involvement of the Head Teacher and the School.

Planning for the large-scale evacuation from London started in May 1938 and is described in the London Metropolitan Archives[68]:-

- In May 1938, the LCC approved the principal of evacuating all its school children.
- July 1938, the Anderson Committee appointed by the Government, reported that evacuation should be voluntary, school parties would be in the care of their teachers and the Government would pay the evacuation costs.
- November 1938 – the Government was preparing the evacuation scheme. See the leaflet below.
- By July 1939, people were privately evacuating from London to the adjoining counties and further afield.
- In July, the Government published a public information leaflet entitled "Evacuation – Why and How".

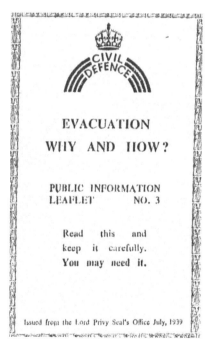

The leaflet contained sections on: -

Why Evacuation?

Details of the Government scheme.

What You Have To Do, covering schoolchildren, children under five, expectant mothers and the blind.

Those making private arrangements.

Some information about the scale of what Sussex would be expected to deal with is contained in a Doctoral thesis by Audrey Elcock[69]:-

---
68 London Metropolitan Archives Information Leaflet Number 32.
69 Government Evacuation Schemes and their effect on schoolchildren.

- Sussex (East and West) could expect to receive about 240,000 evacuees, with West Sussex receiving nearly 85,000.
- In the end, only about 50% of the expected numbers materialised as evacuees.
- By the end of 1939/early in 1940, a large proportion (circa 50%) had returned to their homes in London.

More locally, the West Sussex County Times, almost every week from September 1938, contained articles describing the local arrangements being made to deal with the influx of evacuees. Development of the local scheme was, under the direction of the Home Office, in the hands of an Executive Committee of Horsham Council working with many local voluntary organisations. The starting point for much of their work was the gathering of information and this work is described in a West Sussex County Times article of 20th January 1939, which tells of the work to be done by volunteers.

The arrangements for receiving and processing the evacuees are described in the West Sussex County Times of 1st September 1939[70], in the section entitled "Evacuation Arrangements". The article describes what is planned for Horsham and the surrounding villages: -

- Evacuees would arrive at three rail centres in West Sussex – Horsham, Billingshurst and Crawley.
- Horsham would expect to receive about 10,000 evacuees.
- Planning arrangements for Horsham were under the control of Mr E. Partridge, Horsham's Chief Sanitary Inspector, who will be Chief Billeting Officer. Arrangements for the district, outside Horsham, are under the control of Mr F.F. Haddock, Clerk to the Horsham Rural District Council.
- Horsham had a Rail Head Officer, Mr J. Gell, who was responsible for getting the children safely on board the buses and taking them to the centres where they were to be billeted.

---

70 West Sussex County Times, various articles from September 1938 to September 1939.

Chapter 23: 1939/1945 – *the war years*

London schoolchildren evacuees arriving at Horsham Station on 8th September 1939.

Reception of evacuee children at Horsham Station. Note the top right photo shows a child holding a sign for Sunnyhill School. This is the school from which seven evacuees came who attended Mannings Heath School.

Hilary Dawson[71], a teacher escorting her schoolchildren, wrote a brief remembrance of her arrival in Horsham on that day: -

"What a world this is! We've had such an exciting day; everyone has been most kind and helpful. You should have been at school – farewells etc. – we arrived at Streatham station and got entrained. We did not know until the train stopped at Horsham where we were going.
At Horsham Station there were lots of people to help us with the luggage and also St John's people.
We got in a school bus and were taken a few miles through country lanes. Our school filled three buses and I was the only teacher – with two mothers as helpers in the middle coach.
We arrived finally at Shipley School where another welcome awaited us."

One can imagine that the arrival of the evacuee children, and their teachers, in Nuthurst and Mannings Heath would have evoked similar memories.

The large-scale evacuation, for which there had been much planning, was for the Government Evacuees where the whole, or at least most, of the pupils in a school were evacuated under the supervision of teachers and other helpers. In addition, there were Private Evacuees, and these were youngsters who left London to stay with family relations or with friends outside the capital. There had been a steady "drift" of Private Evacuees from London, to families and friends in Mannings Heath, in the months before the large-scale Government Evacuation.

We are fortunate in having the Evacuee Admissions Register[72] for Mannings Heath School. From this register, we know that, on 11th September 1939, in Mannings Heath, we had the following: -

- Six Government Evacuees from the Woods Road LCC primary school.
- Seven Government Evacuees from the Sunnyhill Road LCC primary school.
- Nine other Government Evacuees from a number of LCC primary schools.
- Eleven Private Evacuees.

The Nuthurst School Head Teacher's Log Book[73] indicates that the total numbers of evacuees was split fairly evenly between St Andrew's and Mannings Heath.

---

71 CEES – Bringing Learning to Life.
72 Evacuee Admissions Register.
73 St Andrews School, Nuthurst Log Book.

Chapter 23: 1939/1945 – *the war years*

The evacuees increased the total number of pupils in Mannings Heath School from thirty-three to fifty-five.

The Government Evacuees were housed: -

- Thirteen at Forest House Childrens Home on Winterpit Lane.
- Three at the Bigg family residence of Swallowfield.
- Two at Ventors Farm, Monks Common.
- Four at other houses that are not specified in the register.

The evacuees were accompanied by a number of their teachers and we have some of their names from the Mannings Heath School log book. Those we have identified are: -

- Cecil Stuart – from Sunnyhill Road School, Streatham who lodged at "The Rest", Worthing Road, Southwater.
- Arthur Giles – from Woods Road School, Southwark who lodged in Comptons Lane, Horsham.
- William Glock – Head of Woods Road School who lodged at "Kirklands", Kings Road, Horsham.
- Mrs Babister – from Woods Road School. Her lodging place is not known.

Sunnyhill Road School, Streatham. It was the first public building to be erected in Streatham in 1901. It was designed to accommodate about 800 junior and infant pupils. In 1901, juniors would be up to 14 years of age.

Woods Road School, Peckham. The school was opened in 1881. It was a primary school for infants and Juniors. It is now the John Donne Primary School and is part of an Academy.

We know a little of what happened on the day of the evacuation from London through an entry in the Head Teacher's Log book for Sunnyhill Road School. The entry reads: -

"The children who were to be evacuated *(not all were evacuated. Some parents denied the advice given and chose to stay in London)* left according to plan. They were in charge of the full staff of teachers in Junior and Infant departments, and all left home for an unknown destination. The train arrived in Horsham, and from there children and staff and helpers were taken to further unknown destinations; one party arrived at Southwater, another at Warnham, another at Ichingfield – villages several miles apart."

It would seem highly probable that the evacuees who arrived in Mannings Heath and Nuthurst were part of the Southwater cohort.

The first entry, by Muriel Howard, in her Head Teacher's Log Book, referring directly to the impact of evacuees on Mannings Heath School, is for Tuesday 12th September 1939. Muriel writes: -

"School for evacuated and local children opened today. The morning session comprised 31 younger children and the afternoon 24 older children. *(This was*

Chapter 23: 1939/1945 – the war years

typical of the teaching in schools which had very big increases in numbers due to the addition of evacuees. They usually split the day with, say, the morning for teaching half the pupils in class whilst the other half went off on a rural pursuit – nature study, farm visit or the like. In the afternoon, the reverse would take place.) Mr Stuart of Sunnyhill Road School, Streatham, reported for duty at 10.00 a.m. Until this morning the Head Teacher *(Muriel Howard)* had not received notification that an assistant teacher was to report to her.

Head Teacher has decided to work the evacuated and local children together. Mr Stuart will take Class 1 consisting of Standards 2 and 3 and the Head Teacher will take Class 2 consisting of Standard 1 and Infants.

From tomorrow Sept 13th onwards, the school will work on a single shift system."

Working a single shift was entirely feasible at Mannings Heath because the school building had two classrooms and had been able to accommodate about eighty pupils in its earlier days.

Despite all the planning, the huge scale of the evacuation meant, inevitably, that there were organisational problems in the early stages.

So, on Tuesday 12th September 1939, we have Mannings Heath School opening for business with the teaching staff consisting of Muriel Howard as the Head Teacher and Cecil Stuart, from Sunnyhill Road, as her assistant.

However, on Friday 15th September, Cecil Stuart told Muriel that he had been recalled to Southwater and that he would be replaced by a teacher currently at Nuthurst School, a Mrs Babister. Muriel tried to find Mrs Babister over the weekend of 16th September but without success. Her Log Book entries contain more than a hint of frustration and she contacted Mr Glock, Mrs Babister's Head Teacher, the appointed Liaison Officer, Mr Brewerton and a Mr Shaw, an Inspector from the LCC but without success. Having heard nothing, Muriel took her own decision and informed the evacuee children not to attend school on Monday 18th September.

It was not until 25th September that Mrs Babister reported to Mannings Heath School and so gradually during that day, the evacuee children returned to the school. Mrs Babister remained teaching at Mannings Heath School until her recall to London on 27th November.

There are two mentions of introducing the "townies" to some country activities. They both came from Frank Dark, a dairy farmer, of Sadlers Farm. Towards the end of October, he had a threshing machine in operation and the whole school spent an afternoon watching the action. Toward the end of November, he paid the school 2s 6d for 2 ½ bushels of acorns the pupils had collected on their various nature walks, to be used as pig feed.

Mrs Babister returned to London on 27th November, leaving the Head Teacher on her own. There had been a steady drift away of the Government evacuees and, by 27th November, only two remained. There were twenty local children and eleven private evacuees, making a total of thirty-three. Muriel was told that it was not possible to provide her with help so she took her own decision to return to the methods of earlier times and re-introduce a version of the old "monitorial" system by using the older, more able children to help groups of younger children with reading and number, and possibly other lessons.

This drift away of the evacuees, and their return to their London homes, was not just specific to Mannings Heath or to Sussex, it was a national phenomenon and it happened despite Government posters and advice for evacuees to stay in the country.

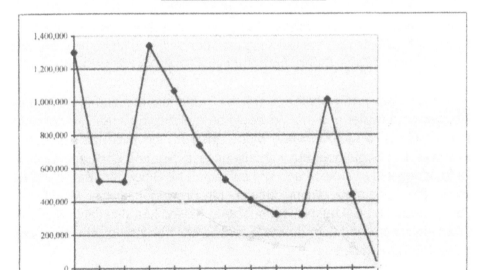

Movements of evacuees under official government schemes during the Second World War

As reported in Ref 69. Government Evacuation Schemes and their effect on children.

The three "peaks" in the overall evacuee movement data coincide with the initial Government evacuation surge in 1939, at the outset of the war, the blitz bombing raids in 1940/41 and the V1/V2 missile attacks following the Allied D

Chapter 23: 1939/1945 – *the war years*

Day landings in 1944.

In Mannings Heath, we saw the number of Government evacuees fall from twenty-two to just one by the end of January 1940. The number of Private Evacuees did not reduce so sharply and remained at between eight and fifteen right through to the end of 1940.

It was not until 18th December that Muriel was given some proper teaching support. On that date Dorothy Woolgar who was, at that time, a West Sussex casual supply teacher, started duties supporting Muriel. Dorothy ultimately became the Head Teacher, overseeing the last days of Mannings Heath School in 1946 – see Appendix 3.

Even though war was underway, Mrs Abbey of Sedgwick Park still provided her Christmas Treat for the children of Nuthurst and Mannings Heath Schools. This year, it was on 20th December 1939 at Nuthurst.

Through 1940, the Head Teacher's Log Book (Ref. 1) records, for the most part, that the school continued to work as it had in peacetime with all the usual illnesses, altercations between pupils, examinations and religious inspections, medical inspections, checking attendance by the Attendance Officer, visits by the Rector, new pupils being admitted and children moving on to senior schools, usually in Horsham.

However, Muriel does describe wartime events in the school which included: -

- Comings and goings of Private and Government Evacuee children (which must have caused problems of arranging continuity of education and meeting the requirements of the LEA syllabuses).
- Additional supplies from the LEA to cater for the increased numbers of pupils.
- Fitting and repair of gas masks.
- Use of the school by the Women's Volunteer Service for first aid meetings.
- The building of an air raid shelter in the playground.
- The provision of blackout curtaining.
- Frequent interruptions to the work of the school from air raid warnings.
- The provision of equipment to deal with incendiary bombs.

The standard, government specified equipment for dealing with incendiary bombs consisted of a scoop, a rake and a container. It was supplemented by graphic "How to" guidance notes.

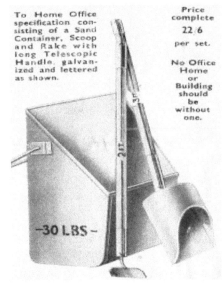

The school was working in an environment of widespread war preparations throughout Sussex. Preparations in Mannings Heath included the construction of pillboxes and anti-tank barricades. We still have the remains of two of the pill boxes, one by the side of the Arun River on Golding Lane and the other on the golf course near to Hammerpond House[74].

---

74 The Pillbox Study Group.

Chapter 23: 1939/1945 – *the war years*

The Golding Lane pillbox is a Type 22 which was designed for use by riflemen. It was about 10ft wide with walls that were between 12 ins and 24 ins thick.

As it may have looked when new.

The pillbox on the golf course is a Type 26. They were classified as "defence posts" and were larger than the Type 22, being about 13ft wide but less substantial, having walls that were no more than 15ins thick.

As it may have looked when new.

We have an eye witness report of anti-tank defences from Judith Browning recorded in Ref 30. She was the great niece of the artist Henry Browning. She records what she describes as a "strange memory" of what she saw in Golding Lane in the high banks going down to the brook. She describes them as "big, black metal barrels with round ends gradually getting overgrown with weeds". We do not know exactly what Judith saw but they were probably a form of anti-tank device, possibly a type of anti-tank cylinder. However, Cliff White[75] offers us more information as, "Large concrete blocks were also in position around the

---

75 The Cliff White Collection – Horsham: The War Years.

village and oil drums filled with petrol were also positioned." It is quite likely that it was these drums that Judith saw in Goldings Lane.

Anti-tank cylinders forming part of the post-Dunkirk defences in England.

Naturally the Log Book concentrates on matters directly related to the school and therefore, does not mention the over two hundred bomb reports throughout Sussex in 1940, although the pupils and the teachers will have been very aware of the enemy bombing and, indeed, of specific incidents near to Mannings Heath that would have had an impact on the lives of the pupils and teachers. Some of these local incidents were: -

- High explosive bombs at the Prongers Corner junction of the Brighton Road and the road to Plummers Plane on 30th September 1939.
- The crash of the Ju 88 bomber at Newells Farm, Nuthurst, on 9th September 1940.
- The crash of the Ju 88 at Lower Beeding on 29th October 1940.
- Seven bombs dropped on Colgate on 9th September 1940, with the loss of five lives.
- Bombs dropped on Orchard Road in Horsham in November with the loss of seven lives.
- The two Halifax bomber crashes at High Beeches and on Mannings Heath Golf Course.
- The huge build-up of Canadian Army units on the Newells estate at Monks Common.

Information about these incidents was a natural by-product of researching for the story of teaching the Heathens and, rather than discard these "by-products", they are included in Appendix 6 as a series of references to sources of more information on the incidents, for those readers who would like to know more.

Chapter 23: 1939/1945 – *the war years*

Throughout 1941, 1942 and 1943, Sussex was becoming one huge army camp with many thousands of Canadian and British troops stationed in camps all over the county. Their presence is well reported in many documents and must have had a big impact on the life of Sussex folk, including school children and on the operation of the schools. However, as described earlier, the Head Teacher's Log Book has barely a mention – just two short entries in the whole log book. The first entry is in June 1942, and is a warning from the local policeman to the children to "keep away from the Cricket Shed on the Common, because it has been taken over by the Army, and the children must not accept gifts from the Canadian soldiers." The second entry is in May 1943, and tells us that a pupil – John Button – was knocked down by a Canadian Army lorry when running across Golding Lane from the Common to the School. He was not badly hurt.

These two entries show us a little of the Canadian Army presence, and that of other military units, in and around Mannings Heath, but do not give any real idea of the scale of the Canadian, and British, Army activities in the local area nor any real idea of West Sussex as a "garrison county". Alan Readman in his "Story of the Home Front"[76] paints a vivid picture of happenings throughout the county, including the Canadian Army, British troops under General Montgomery, visits by Winston Churchill... - see Appendix 6 which gives references to information sources for more details.

What this author finds remarkable is that, in the midst of what must have been a maelstrom of military activity from 1942 to mid-1944, this activity had so small a reported impact on the everyday life of Mannings Heath and its school, as recorded by the Head Teacher. So, to get a more rounded picture, we need to look at various personal reminiscences from the local population, and we are fortunate to have two good sources: -

- Reference 39 – Memories of Mannings Heath, compiled and edited by Tony Turner.
- Reference 75 – The Cliff White Collection, compiled and edited by Cliff White.

The Mannings Heath policeman during the war was P.C. Joe Lemm. He, and his wife Kathleen and their two young children, lived in the Police House on the Brighton Road, opposite the Old Post House. He recalled that: -

- He came close to prosecuting the Rector for consistently not having a good blackout.

---

[76] The Story of the Home front in West Sussex 1939-1945.

- Actually nicking (his word) locals who did not obey the "business only" regulations for motor car use and who used their cars for trips to the pub and to the golf club.
- Plane crashes at Newells Farm, Studs Farm, Plummers Plain and Cooks Farm and doodlebugs (V1) at Colgate and Swallowfield.

P.C. Joe Lemm in the garden of the Police House.

Gilbert Newberry, who lived at Winterpick Cottage tells of: -

- The local Mannings Heath Auxilliary Fire Service, with its base in a hut opposite the Dun Horse pub. There were ten members, and he was one of those, and they were on duty twenty-four hours a day in three shifts.
- They were called out to plane crashes, bomb explosions and flying bomb incidents.
- They started off with just a hand pump, but latterly were equipped with a Coventry Climax trailer pump, probably when they became incorporated into the National Fire Service and became directed from Horsham.

Chapter 23: 1939/1945 – *the war years*

The Canadian Army North Novas, based at Monks Common, were a continual military presence in and around Mannings Heath. They: -

- Were often "on manoeuvres" around the village with Canadians, dressed in German uniforms, playing the part of the enemy.
- Were keen supporters of Mannings Heath Golf Club and provided a regular income source to local lads who found golf balls and sold them back to their original owners.
- Had frequent parades and marches, with pipes and drums playing; sometimes into Horsham on special occasions.

There were a number of enemy and British aircraft crashes around Mannings Heath described by various locals in Refs. 39 and 75, and in other sources, that must have been major local events affecting, and fascinating, the school pupils and teachers, but none get a mention in the Head Teacher's Log Book for the period, which attempts to convey an image of relative normality among the community and in the life of the school.

Apart from the continuing presence of large numbers of troops at Monks Common, there are many reports, in a number of sources, of aircraft crashes and explosions in and around Mannings Heath, and all of them must have excited a mixture of fear and curiosity among the Mannings Heath school children, and certainly added colour to the life of the village.

Returning to the life of the school and the Log Book for 1941, we find that, perhaps better late than never, arrangements were being made for the supply and hanging of black-out curtains and gas mask wearing practices were being held.

The total number on the school role was thirty-three, of which seven were evacuees.

As a sign of the "normality" of village life, despite the war, the school was closed in August for the usual annual flower and produce show.

It was in August 1941, that the Headmistress, Muriel Howard, left after seven years as Head.

As well as her interest in photography, Muriel had a keen interest in British birds and, as a token of their appreciation, the children made a presentation to Muriel of the beautifully illustrated "British Birds" by Kirkman and Jourdain.

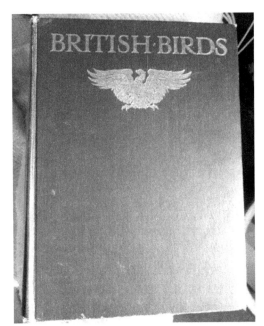 

The book was inscribed with the message "Miss Howard – with kind remembrances and best wishes from the children of Mannings Heath School".

Muriel was replaced by Marjorie Sharp for the start of the Autumn term in October 1941. "Sharp" was, in fact, her maiden name which she continued to use for her professional life. Her married name was Bussey – she had married Alan Bussey, a County Court Clerk, in the second quarter of 1941, about six months before taking up her appointment as Head Teacher at Mannings Heath. In November, there were thirty-three children on the roll with just seven being the few remaining evacuees.

Majorie's first action was to seek the removal of the school air raid shelter that had been built in the playground; the reason was that it was collapsing under its own weight, with no help from the enemy. Randalls, a local contractor, filled in the trench in March 1942. Marjorie also petitioned the LEA for an additional heating stove; the winter had been exceptionally cold.

The Biggs continued their interest in the school and visited frequently, usually bringing small gifts of books and crayons. Mrs Abbey of Sedgwick visited at Christmas with the Rector, acting as Santa, to hand out small presents of toys and sweets to each child.

In November 1939, the Ministry of Supply set up a special Directorate for Salvage and Local Authorities, such as Horsham, were required to submit targets for the recovery of metals, waste paper and waste rubber; targets were supported by an advertising campaign and by competitions to see who could collect the most.

One of the Ministry of Supply advertisements to encourage the collection of metal, paper, rubber and bone salvage.

In January 1942, Mannings Heath School took part in a competition organised by Horsham RDC for paper collection, and they won by collecting 2,990 lbs (or 1.3 tons) of scrap paper in the month of January. This was the equivalent of over 93 lbs collected by each pupil – remarkable!

It was in June 1942 that PC Lemm spoke to the school and warned the children to keep away from the cricket shed on the Common as it had been taken over for use by the Army (probably the Canadians based at Monks Common). He also warned the children against accepting gifts from the Canadian soldiers. But we do know that the Canadians made use of Mannings Heath Golf Club and that some children supplemented their pocket money by finding golf balls and selling them back to the Canadians. There is no record of that practice coming to an end despite the warning from PC Lemm!

In September there were twenty-eight pupils on the register and Dorothy Woolgar was working as a supply teacher and assistant to the Head Teacher,

Marjorie Sharp. The WVS were making plans for the school to act as a Rest Centre for those who were local victims of the war. Later in the year (in November), the school was used as a centre for the registration of volunteers for fire watching duties in Mannings Heath.

Also, in November, Marjorie Sharp resigned as Head Teacher, effective from 31st December, and Dorothy was appointed as Temporary Head, pending the appointment of a replacement for Marjorie. And, just to round off the year on a high, the school cloakroom flooded and Randalls, the builders, were called in to do the necessary repairs.

However, on a more festive note, Mrs Abbey gave her annual Christmas party for the pupils at St Andrew's School in Nuthurst.

1943 started with Dorothy Woolgar as Temporary Head Teacher whilst a permanent replacement was found. Edith Sanderson joined Mannings Heath School as Head in February and, at that point, Dorothy Woolgar reverted to her Assistant role.

March saw a devastating air disaster which led to the destruction of High Beedches, the home of the Loder family. References to information on this event are in Appendix 6 and, although not mentioned in the Log Book, the scale of the relatively local disaster must have made a real impression on the residents of Mannings Heath.

In April 1943, there was a real innovation in school operations – the first Parents meeting was held. There were twenty-five pupils on the register, with one evacuee still at the school. A second innovation took place in May and June when the school was provided with its own radio and BBC engineers arrived to install it and put it into operation.

The Diocesan Inspection that took place in June was a big success, with Edith being described as a "keen, young teacher".

In November, the school was equipped with a stove and urn so that canteen dinners could be provided for staff and pupils and, as usual, the year ended with Mrs Abbey's Christmas Party, with films and a Father Christmas, held at St Andrew's School.

Locally, 1944 was dominated by air raids and air raid warnings caused by V1 attacks on the South-East of England, and the schools in Mannings Heath and in Nuthurst spent much time sheltering as a result of alerts. On 21st July there were

Chapter 23: 1939/1945 – *the war years*

four alerts during the school day. The standing instructions to the children were to "take shelter under the desks in the event of an air raid warning". And, on 1st August, it happened for real with a V1 in Winterpit Lane. No one in the school was injured, but windows were blown in and plaster ceilings brought down.

The National Union of Teachers, founded in 1888, made its first recorded recruitment attempts in Mannings Heath when, in February, a representative visited the school and attempted to recruit the two teachers, neither of whom were in the Union. The Log Book does not record whether or not the attempt was successful. But the fact that it happened was a sign of things to come.

In March, Dorothy Woolgar was appointed as a Temporary Assistant Teacher and, at last, two efficient stoves were provided to give more effective heating than the open fires.

By the end of 1944 all the evacuees had returned home and the number of the roll was down to twenty-six. In December, the Head Teacher resigned – we do not know the reason but it was probably due to the falling number of pupils and the possible closure which, although not announced at that time, was becoming ever more likely.

As a result of the resignation, Dorothy Woolgar was acting as Head Teacher again, and was working alone in this capacity.

And, indeed, in February 1945, a letter was received from the Education Office advising of a possible closure of the Junior Department (essentially the older children - those between 8 and 11 years of age). The parents were asked if their child could go to Lower Beeding School. In fact, the parents began to act on their own initiative to get their children into other schools of their choice.

On 16th February, the following transfers were agreed and, on 5th June, the Junior Department was officially closed.

Pupil Name	Register No.	Age	Transferred to
John Martin	804	11	Denne Road
Robin King	799	10	Denne Road
Gwen Ford	816	8	St Mary's
Anna Britten	821	8	St Mary's
Sheila Brown	803	11	Oxford Road

Pupil Name	Register No.	Age	Transferred to
Pamela Turrell	813	8	Victory Road
Derek Dollard	830	9	Lower Beeding
Charlie Jenner	814	9	Lower Beeding
Edward Grummitt	827	8	Lower Beeding
Daphne Sheppard	805	9	Lower Beeding

With other leavers, the number on the register was reduced to just thirteen by the end of June.

The Log Book records that, on 8th and 9th May, the school had an extra two days holiday to celebrate the victory in Europe; this seems to have been the extent of the school celebration of the event.

In October 1945, it became clear to the Managers that both St Andrew's in Nuthurst and Mannings Heath School were under threat of closure. The Minutes of the Managers Meeting for 24th October record that "The Rector expressed the concern of the Managers at the situation at both schools. Mannings Heath had already been "black listed" for closure but he was prepared to do all possible to retain Nuthurst as a Church School. It would possibly cost between £2,000 and £5,000 to bring the school *(presumably St Andrew's)* up to the requirements of the New Education Act, and the LEA would be asking for the managers plans. The Rector commented that the fact of numbers had to be faced – there were only 7 children in the school. *(This was a reference to Mannings Heath School)."*

The Minutes of the Managers Meeting on 27th December record that, "The Education Authorities had decided to close Mannings Heath School temporarily and arrange for the children to attend Lower Beeding but that an extension of time to Easter, 1946 had been granted". The minutes go on to record that, "The School, School House and Church Hall were all built on land given by Trust Deed for Church use; which, if it ceased to be used for Church purposes would probably revert to the Scrace Dickins family as the original owners".

So, at the end of 1945, there was real concern in the Parish of Nuthurst that the Parish could lose both of its schools and the use of the land on which Mannings Heath School, the School House and the village hall were built.

Chapter 24

The End – *1946 and after*

1946 started with all the usual school routines, albeit for just one class of eight pupils. There were visits from the nurse with "head inspections", weekly visits by the Education Authority Attendance Officer, visits from the Rector to check the register and to take lessons, the usual list of pupil sicknesses – bronchitis, whooping cough, broken bones etc. In other words, school life, at this reduced scale, held all the usual elements.

But appearances were deceptive. Dorothy Woolgar was invited to attend a meeting of the school Managers on 2nd April. She was formally advised that Mannings Heath School was to be closed by the Local Education Authority (LEA) at the end of the Summer term.

However, Dorothy told the Managers that Mannings Heath parents had raised a petition to the LEA to keep the school open and the petition had attracted fifty signatures – not bad for a school with eight pupils on its register. The reply from the LEA had been, as expected, that the school was not economic for the number of children.

It is perhaps worth remembering that it was the earlier actions of the LEA itself, in the 1920s, and in the 1940s, that had led to the pupil numbers being radically reduced and led to the "uneconomic" label being attached in 1946.

Dorothy told the Managers that, if the school was to be closed, the parents wished the remaining pupils to attend St Andrew's School in Nuthurst and that she was willing to be seconded to teach at St Andrew's – and not to Lower Beeding as had been suggested on earlier occasions by the LEA.

Nothing to do with the school, but there was excitement in Mannings Heath in April 1946, with the escape of German Prisoners of War from their camp in Billingshurst. They had managed to make their way to Mannings Heath but, according to the West Sussex Gazette, were "confronted by some local men, who were out vermin hunting with shot guns, and handed over to the police".

One of the POWs, named Rehaag, was a serial escaper and was described as being on his third escape.

On 28th June 1946, matters regarding the school closure were formalised in a letter from the LEA stating that: "After closure at the end of this term, the pupils will be conveyed to Nuthurst and Mrs Woolgar will be appointed to fill the vacancy at Nuthurst School".

The term end date was 26th July 1946, and it dawned overcast and humid. Much of July had been very hot with temperatures in the 80s; not at all pleasant to be cooped up in a school classroom. Later on in the day, the rain came and it poured, with about two inches falling in just half an hour, according to the Met Office records. The rain was accompanied by rumbles of thunder forming a slightly ominous accompaniment to the final closure of Mannings Heath School after 63 years of teaching over 800 pupils.

At three o'clock, Dorothy Woolgar said goodbye to the six remaining pupils and promised to see four of them next term at St Andrew's, Nuthurst. She cleared the papers from her desk and, on leaving, looked across at the Common, where so many of her charges had played, before locking the school door, for the last time as the Head Teacher, and setting off for her home in Monks Gate.

Dorothy's view across the Common on leaving Mannings Heath School.

Epilogue

For the first week of the 1946 Autumn term, Dorothy spent time clearing up the school building before it was made available to William Randall & Co., a Horsham builder, for use as an office and store. The school playground was used as a children's playground. In the early 1950s, the building was knocked down and the plot used for the construction of two bungalows, Hilldor and Green Leaves.

So, a sad end to at least 120 years of "teaching the Heathens" in Mannings Heath.

Or was it? Well, no, not quite.

Our Mannings Heath story started with the Methodists and the Sunday School, in their first Chapel, in the 1830s. The reader of this story, who has stayed the distance, will have picked up that the Methodist contribution to teaching the Heathens in Sunday School had never ceased and that the Church of England school had lived happily alongside Methodist worship in the Chapel, C of E worship in the Church of the Good Shepherd and the Methodist Sunday School. Indeed, a fine example of ecumenism in practice. The records of our "Heathens" show many examples of baptisms as Methodists and, subsequently, a wedding in St Andrew's church, with attendance at both the C of E school and Methodist Sunday schools in between.

I am indebted to a member of the Horsham Methodist Chapel for a personal note describing the following events concerning the re-emergence of the Mannings Heath Methodist Sunday School and the continuing contribution from the Methodist congregation to "Teaching the Heathens".

By 1962, membership amongst Mannings Heath Methodists had dwindled and the Christmas Service in 1962 marked the closure of the Chapel opposite the two bungalows that had replaced the school building and playground.

In 1967, David Ansell, a Methodist Local Preacher from Horsham, visited Mannings Heath and spoke to children playing on the Common. He asked them if they would come to a Sunday School if one was opened in the village. They said they would and this was enough for David to seek permission from the Methodist Circuit to re-open the Chapel. So, a gang of Methodist members of the Horsham Chapel set about work to clean up and repair the Mannings Heath Chapel and to prepare it for re-opening.

In March 1968, a re-opening service was held under the leadership of Rev. Ronald Rawlings, the Circuit Superintendent. The preacher was Rev. Paul Bishop from the Horsham, Brighton Road Baptist Church and he used "Behold, I lay before you an open door, which no man can shut" (Revelation 3:8) as his very appropriate text.

A Sunday School was started in the re-opened Chapel and it continued until the dwindling number of regular worshippers forced the Chapel Trustees to sell it in 1972 as a private residence. The Sunday School continued but moved to the third (after the two Chapels) centre of Methodism in Mannings Heath at the National Children's Home at Forest House in Winterpit Lane, Mannings Heath.

Forest House was a large country house in 12 acres of land and, before the Methodists moved in, was the property of the Lutwyche family, headed by Gerald Lutwyche until, in 1951, it was opened as one of the Methodist National Children's Homes. The National Children's Home movement was started by the Rev. Thomas Stephenson in a disused stable block in Exton Street, London, as a response to his shock at the plight of homeless children on the streets of London in 1869.

The Children's Home at Forest House was unique. It was set up as a specialist nursery for some twenty very young children suffering from pulmonary tuberculosis, and it was the only such specialised treatment centre in England. As time went by, it changed to a more conventional Children's Home, with the older children in three family groups with each group under the care of a team of trained and student nursery nurses. Many of the babies, when well, and the younger children, were adopted and left the home. In the 1980s, the head was Mrs Angel and her deputy was Mrs Godby. Children of primary school age from the Home went to St Andrew's School in Nuthurst.

Epilogue

Forest House National Childrens Home, Winterpit Lane, Mannings Heath.

The Sunday School moved to the Village Hall and became more "non-denominational" to widen its appeal. It continued to be run by Methodist volunteers into the 1980s.

The personal note to which I referred ends with the following: -

"The object of the Sunday School is to present the Gospel of the Lord Jesus Christ, so that the children and their families have the opportunity of believing in and knowing Him as their Lord and Saviour. Please pray for us."

In the Introduction to this story of Teaching the Heathens, I made reference to acts of generosity by members of the community, and I can think of no better example than the continued commitment of the Methodist community to the teaching of the Heathens.

At the start of this project, I envisaged that I would be writing about a 63-year period – being the life of Mannings Heath School from 1883 to 1946. In fact, the story that has come to light has revealed a picture of 150 years in the life of a Sussex village and its children.

On a personal note, it has been a fascinating and enlightening journey for this novice author.

Appendix 1

The Chart Family Genealogy – 1770s to 1940s

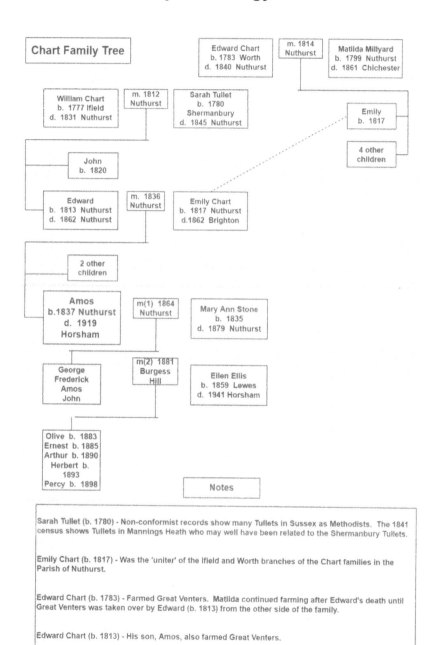

Sarah Tullet (b. 1780) - Non-conformist records show many Tullets in Sussex as Methodists. The 1841 census shows Tullets in Mannings Heath who may well have been related to the Shermanbury Tullets.

Emily Chart (b. 1817) - Was the 'uniter' of the Ifield and Worth branches of the Chart families in the Parish of Nuthurst.

Edward Chart (b. 1783) - Farmed Great Venters. Matilda continued farming after Edward's death until Great Venters was taken over by Edward (b. 1813) from the other side of the family.

Edward Chart (b. 1813) - His son, Amos, also farmed Great Venters.

Amos Chart (b. 1837) - Farmer, road surveyor and Horsham merchant. Trustee, leader and staunch supporter of the Mannings Heath Methodist community, school and chapels.

Appendix 2

Record of Pupils Joining the Mannings Heath C.E./Board School in the First Academic Years 1883/4 & 1884/5

Data transcribed from the Mannings Heath School Register of Admissions, Progress and Withdrawal, 1883-1946.

Held by the West Sussex Record Office, Chichester with the school log books as refs. E143B/12/1, 2 and 3.

Name	Age	From	Standard on arrival	Standard on leaving	Leaving date
Alfred Highgate	11	Mannings Heath	4	5	25/05/84
Thomas Highgate	9	Mannings Heath	2	3	01/06/88
William Highgate	7	Mannings Heath	1	3	22/06/88
James Highgate	5	Mannings Heath	0	3	13/11/89
Alice Blackwell	6	Mannings Heath	1	3	16/10/85
James Blackwell	6	Mannings Heath	0	3	07/08/90
Harry Ansell	13	Mannings Heath	0	1	23/11/89
Alfred Ansell	8	Mannings Heath	4	4	30/05/84
Charles Ashford	13	Little Ventors Farm	1	3	22/10/86
James Ashford	11	Little Ventors Farm	0	No record	14/03/84
Mary Ashford	6	Little Ventors Farm	0	No record	06/12/84
Florence Ashford	7	Little Ventors Farm	0	No record	24/03/85
Frederick Budgen	5	Whitings Farm	0	3	30/05/88
George Boniface	7	Monks Common	0	1	06/08/86
Emma Attwater	8	Mannings Heath	0	3	05/11/86
Grace Botting	12	Mannings Heath	4	No record	22/02/84
Eliza Burchell	11	Mannings Heath	2	No record	25/05/84
Allen Budgen	6	Whitings Farm	0	4	30/05/88

Appendix 2: Record of Pupils Joining the Mannings Heath C.E./Board School

Name	Age	From	Standard on arrival	Standard on leaving	Leaving date
Celia Botting	6	Mannings Heath	0	4	24/02/88
Alfred Flint	10	Mannings Heath	3	5	18/01/86
Henry Francis	11	Rickfield Farm	2	4	25/05/84
Alice Francis	9	Rickfield Farm	0	4	15/06/88
John Gatland	9	Mannings Heath	1	No record	17/08/85
Henry Heasman	12	Mannings Heath	0	1	26/10/86
Ephriam Heasman	5	Mannings Heath	0	3	30/01/91
Jesse Heasman	4	Mannings Heath	0	3	15/06/91
Minnie Holford	11	Sun Oak	0	4	23/06/86
Agnes Holford	7	Sun Oak	0	4	17/08/88
Kate Jupp	11	Mannings Heath	3	4	23/05/84
Ruth Jupp	4	Mannings Heath	0	2	15/06/91
Robert Lewry	9	Monks Common	1	3	23/03/87
Ellen Laker	9	Mannings Heath	1	3	29/07/87
Clive Lewry	13	Monks Common	0	4	17/10/87
Mary Lewry	6	Monks Common	0	5	17/05/89
Ernest Mitchell	8	Birchen Bridge	1	6	29/07/87
Fanny Mason	11	Mannings Heath	4	5	17/08/85

Name	Age	From	Standard on arrival	Standard on leaving	Leaving date
Florence Mitchell	9	Birchen Bridge	0	4	17/07/85
Harry Nicholson	6	Mannings Heath	0	4	26/10/88
Jane Nicholson	13	Mannings Heath	0	2	25/06/87
Caroline Nicholson	4	Mannings Heath	0	1	14/12/91
Bertie Lintott	13	St Leonards F'rst	4	5	16/04/85
Stanley Rowland	9	Mannings Heath	0	5	22/06/88
Nelson Rowland	6	Mannings Heath	0	3	14/03/90
George Redford	?	Colgate	0	No record	25/05/84
Ernest Redford	4	Colgate	0	No record	01/08/84
Alice Redford	?	Colgate	0	No record	01/08/84
Edward Knight	8	Mannings Heath	1	No record	25/08/85
Jane Knight	11	Mannings Heath	4	No record	25/05/84
Caroline Knight	6	Mannings Heath	0	4	11/06/88
Thomas Thorns	7	Mannings Heath	0	4	23/12/87
William Thorns	4	Mannings Heath	0	5	29/05/90
Annie Thorns	11	Mannings Heath	4	No record	30/05/84
Edward Thorns	3	Mannings Heath	0	2	01/07/92
William Wells	11	Birchen Bridge	4	6	04/06/86

Appendix 2: Record of Pupils Joining the Mannings Heath C.E./Board School

Name	Age	From	Standard on arrival	Standard on leaving	Leaving date
Lilian Wickens	12	Mannings heath	4	6	25/05/84
Emma Wickens	10	Mannings Heath	2	4	31/01/87
Helen Wells	9	Birchen Bridge	0	5	29/07/86
Louisa Wickens	7	Mannings Heath	0	4	24/12/90
Claude Worcester	6	Mannings Heath	0	2	05/11/86
Ellen Worcester	5	Mannings Heath	0	6	29/05/93
Fred Lewry	4	Mannings Heath	0	4	26/04/92
Rosa Boniface	12	Mannings Heath	No record	No record	25/05/84
Charles Holford	4	Sun Oak	No record	2	28/04/92

Appendix 3
Mannings Heath C.E./Board School

The Head Teachers

Data extracted from the School Head Teachers Log Books held by the West Sussex Record Office, Chichester as refs. E143B/12/1, 2 and 3.

Cited as Reference 1 and from a range of other sources.

Mannings Heath School

Head Teachers

Start/Finish	Name	Notes
Sept. 1883/ Dec. 1884	Annie Farrer	First Head Teacher who opened the school on 10th Sept. Born in 1858, the daughter of a Kendal, Westmorland farmer. She returned to Kendal to continue teaching and to marry John Swindenbank in 1899. She died in Kendal in 1935.
Jan. 1885/ Aug. 1885	Annie Harwood	Certificated, young teacher from Doncaster. Mannings Heath was a promotion for her to a Head Teacher position. After Mannings Heath, she returned to Yorkshire to continue her teaching career.
Sept. 1885/ Feb. 1886	Louisa Buck	She was born in 1849 in Silverton, Devon, and was the daughter of an Excise Officer. She came to Mannings Heath from a teaching position in Honiton, Devon. Resigned to take up a better position. See Chapter 9 for more detail.
Mar. 1886/ Jan. 1887	Rosina Williams	Was the first occupant of the new School House provided by Augusta Bigg. Dismissed by Rev J McCarogher on 11th Jan. Refused to admit a pupil.
Feb. 1887/ May 1887	Miss Turner	Engaged on a temporary, three-month contract.

Appendix 3: Mannings Heath C.E./Board School

May 1887/ May 1913	Louisa Reading (nee Buck)	Returned as Head Teacher on 9th May, having married William Reading on 27th April in Nuthurst Church. William was Head of the earlier Methodist school and continued teaching at Mannings Heath School as Assistant Master. They lived in the School House until Louisa retired when they moved to Hollands. See Chapter 9 for more detail.
May 1913/ Nov. 1913	A number of temporary and supply teachers in charge of the school.	
Dec. 1913/ July 1915	Eliza Blanche Titterton – always known as Blanche.	Born in Shifnal, Shropshire, in 1868. Her father, John, had a large farm, The Manor Farm, of about 250 acres. She trained as a teacher and started teaching in Shifnal before becoming a Head Teacher in Salford Priors, Warwickshire. She died in Weston Super Mare in 1953.
Sept. 1915/ Feb. 1918	Elsie Marion Wood- always known as Marion	Born in Peckham, London, as the daughter of a gold mining company clerk/company secretary. She qualified in 1914 and Mannings Heath was her first teaching appointment. She left the school due to illness and on medical advice.
Feb. 1918/ Nov. 1918	A number of temporary and supply teachers.	

Nov. 1918/ March 1925	Gertrude Ellis	Gertrude Annie Ellis was born in 1867, the daughter of William and Elsie Ellis from Scotland. By the age of 14, she was no longer living with her parents but was the ward of David and Eliza Munro, also from Scotland, and was living in Poplar, London. By the time she was 24, she was an Assistant Mistress at a school in Tower Hamlets. She became a qualified (certificated) teacher sometime around 1900 and was teaching in a Camden Town school in 1911 before coming to her first Headship in Mannings Heath in 1918 when she was 51 and where she remained until 1925. Gertrude died in Peckham, London, in September 1938, at the age of 71.
April 1925/ July 1931	Amy W Unwins	Born in 1899, the daughter of George Unwins, who was a nurseryman in Merrow, Guildford. In the December school holiday of 1929, she married Robert Lewin in Horsham. She died in Uckfield in 1944.
Sept. 1931/ Dec. 1933	E. Olive Lewry	Born in 1908 as the third child of Kate and John Lewry, a gardener of Homefields, Cowfold. She became Head Teacher of a Littlehampton School, after leaving Mannings Heath, whilst living at 9 Connaught Road, Littlehampton. She died in Crawley in 1985.

Appendix 3: Mannings Heath C.E./Board School

Jan. 1934/ Sept. 1941	Muriel Amy Howard	Muriel was born in Chichester on 28th October 1911. She was the daughter of Charlie Howard, who was a photographer working in Chichester and living at 12 North Street. Muriel was trained at Bishop Otter College (now part of Chichester University). She probably qualified in 1930 as a teacher, so Mannings Heath School was likely to have been her second appointment. In September 1941, she joined the teaching staff of Walberton School near Chichester. She never married and worked at Walberton until her retirement in 1971. Whilst teaching in Mannings Heath she lived at Frederick House in Monks Gate. She died in Chichester on 3rd May 1989.
Oct. 1941/ Dec. 1942	Marjorie E Sharp	Marjorie was born in December, 1916, the daughter of a Hastings inn keeper. In the second quarter of 1941 she married Alan Bussey, a County Court Clerk in Hastings and, at the time, she was an Assistant Elementary Teacher in Hastings. She had been married about six months before taking up her Mannings Heath appointment. She continued to use her maiden name whilst teaching and she died in Dover in 1997.
Feb. 1943/ Dec. 1944	Edith Muriel Sanderson	Edith was born in Wigtown, Cumberland in April 1899 and trained as a teacher at Warrington Training College. She started her teaching career as an Assistant Mistress in Aspatria, Allerdale, Cumberland, in 1920.

Jan. 1943/ July 1946	Dorothy E Woolgar 	Joined Mannings Heath School in December 1939, as a Supply Teacher, helping out with the increased numbers of evacuee pupils. She became temporary Head Teacher in 1942 following the departure of Marjorie Sharp until the arrival of Edith Page. On the departure of Edith Page she became Head and oversaw declining pupil numbers and the closure of the school at the end of the 1946 school year. She transferred, as a teacher, to St Andrew's School in Nuthurst. Dorothy was born Dorothy Suter in 1901. She was the daughter of Amos Suter, a Horsham Police Sergeant. The Suter family moved to North Mundam, Chichester, on Amos's retirement. Dorothy married Archie Woolgar, a painter and decorator, in 1927 and moved to 8 Nuthurst Road, Monks Gate. She died in Horsham in 1961.

Appendix 4

Mannings Heath School Pupils Who Saw Military Service in World War 1

Name	Date of Birth	Year of School Entry	Register Number	Age on Leaving
Albert Barnard	02/02/80	1893	258	12
Son of Edward Barnard. Left school with a Labour Certificate so could seek employment. Reached Standard 3. Thought to have served as a Driver in the Royal Field Artillery, service number 97944.				
Reuben Barnard	02/02/97	1900	355	7
Son of Edward Barnard and brother of Albert. Served in Army Labour Corps as a Private. Service number 672781.				
Charles Boniface	13/12/75	1883	3	13
Joined Mannings Heath School at its opening. Previously at St Andrew's, Nuthurst. Nearly 40 years old at start of WW1. Thought to have served in Army Labour Corps. Service number 360881.				
William Boniface	09/05/78	1882	82	7
Lived at Monks Common. Probably younger brother of Charles. Thought to have served as Acting Corporal in Royal Sussex Regiment. Service number GSSR/25.				
John Cox	12/06/93	1898	335	5
Came from Rickfield Farm and left the village, but presumably not the Parish, after he had been at Mannings Heath School for only a few months.				
Albert Gatland	17/10/94	1897	324	14
Son of James Gatland of Mannings Heath. Was employed after leaving school. Thought to have served in the Army Labour Corps. Service number 569166				

John Gatland	15/08/94	1904	40	11
Came from Readings School in the first Methodist Chapel. Was promoted to Sergeant but died on active service.				
Fred Glaysher	07/02/95	1898	337	13
Came from Rugby Road School in Preston. Achieved his Labour Certificate so could seek employment on leaving school. Served in the 12th Battalion of the Royal Sussex Regiment. Service number G/17842. Died aged 20.				
William Glaysher	04/07/98	1892	322	13
Achieved his Labour Certificate and could seek employment on leaving school. Served in the 9th Battalion of the Royal Sussex Regiment. Service number 201445C. Reported missing at Messines in June 1917. Headstone in Nuthurst Church Yard.				
John Glaysher	04/07/97	1900	369	13
Achieved his Labour Certificate and was employed after leaving school. Served as a Gunner in the Royal Field Artillery. Service number L11773.				
Ronald Glaysher	07/06/00	1904	408	12
Achieved his Labour Certificate and was employed in his parents' business on leaving school. No record found of his service unit.				
Picton Highgate	04/07/97	1900	362	12
Achieved his Labour Certificate. Served with the 7th Battalion, Royal Sussex Regiment. Awarded the DCM and MM with two bars. Service number 3833.				
William Highgate	10/05/74	1883	6	14
Came from Reading's School in the first Methodist Chapel. Achieved Standard 3 at Mannings Heath School. Thought to have served as a Gunner in the Royal Artillery. Service number 111800.				
Thomas Jupp	15/03/91	1894	280	12
Achieved Standard 4 and his Labour Certificate. Was awarded the DCM and MM. Promoted to Sergeant. Served in 6 Divisional Signal Company of Royal Engineers. Service number 23159.				
William Jupp	31/12/94	1899	356	8
Brother of Thomas. Left service due to ill health; had an operation in Brighton Hospital. Was Christened as a Methodist.				
Frederick Knight	24/03/96	1900	211	12

Appendix 4: Mannings Heath School Pupils Who Saw Military Service

Name	DOB	Year left	Admission no.	Age left
\multicolumn{5}{	l	}{Son of James Knight. Achieved Standard 5. In employment after leaving school.}
Harry Mitchell	10/02/00	1904	445	14
\multicolumn{5}{	l	}{Came from St Andrew's School, Nuthurst, to Mannings Heath School. No service details found.}
Frederick Richardson	01/01/92	2895	284	12
\multicolumn{5}{	l	}{Achieved his Labour Certificate. Private in the Royal Sussex Regiment. Service number L/10133. Served with his brother, Forester. Died on active service at Ypres on 24th October 1914. Recorded on Menin Gate Memorial.}
Forester Richardson	26/08/97	1900	365	12
\multicolumn{5}{	l	}{Served as a Driver in the Royal Field Artillery. Service number 94847. After the war, became a well digger. His family lived on the land which subsequently became The Nook on Church Road.}
William Richardson	15/11/94	1897	327	13
\multicolumn{5}{	l	}{Achieved his Labour Certificate. No service details found.}
Charles Simpson	05/05/96	1908	476	12
\multicolumn{5}{	l	}{Came from East Parade School, Horsham. Only at Mannings Heath School for three months. No service details found.}
Edward Thorns	29/12/80	1883	70	12
\multicolumn{5}{	l	}{Was at Readings School. Thought to have served in the Army Labour Corps. Service number 461318.}
Walter Venn	12/07/83	1888	162	12
\multicolumn{5}{	l	}{Lived at Monks Common. Achieved Standard 5. Served as a Gunner in the Royal Field Artillery. Service number 161409.}
George Warman	Not known	Not known	165	12(?)
\multicolumn{5}{	l	}{A "Deserted Child" admitted from Croydon Union under the care of Henry Warman. Thought to have served in the Army Labour Corps. Service number 88668.}
Ernest Worcester	12/04/91	1895	282	12

Achieved Standard 4 and his Labour Certificate. Lance Corporal in the Royal Sussex Regiment. Service number SD5345. During WW1, corresponded with William Reading, his old teacher.				
Lennard Worcester	29/12/93	1898	340	14
Achieved his Labour Certificate. Thought to have served in the Army Pay Corps. Service number 14313.				
Leslie Worcester	24/01/98	1901	372	6
Left school early due to ill health. Thought to have served as a Gunner in 126 Brigade of the Royal Field Artillery. Service number 172242. Wounded in service.				
Not recorded on the Memorial but was at Mannings heath School and served in WW1				
Ernest Cowdry	21/12/90	1894	271	13
Achieved his Labour Certificate. Served in the Worcester and Hampshire Regiments. The family lived at Ivy Cottage and his mother, Louisa, was the caretaker at the Mission Church. Ernest corresponded with William Reading, his teacher, during the war.				

Appendix 5

Pupil Numbers on the School Register

Data extracted from The Pupil Register (part of Reference 1), the Head Teacher Log Books (part of Reference 1) and documents in the National Archives (see Reference 66)

Year	Pupils on Register	Notes
1885	75	Includes those transferred from Reading's School.
1890	63	
1900	60	
1905	60	Of whom 18 were classed as Infants.
1910	52	Of whom 12 were classed as Infants.
1915	34	WW1 had an effect on numbers on Register. Perhaps due to families moving away.
1920	57	At the start of the arguments about closing the school. All as recorded in Reference 66. See Chapter 19.
1923	55	In June. Pupil numbers from the Log Book.
1925	23	As a result of the outcome of the arguments in Reference 66 which resulted in all Mannings Heath children over 10 years of age being educated at St Andrew's, Nuthurst, or other local schools.
1930	18	All 10 years of age or less.
1932	23	
1933	25	
1935	26	

Year	Pupils on Register	Notes
1936	20	
1938	23	
1939	55	Made up of local children and evacuees from London County Council schools and other, private, evacuees staying with local residents.
1942	28	Most of the evacuees had returned to their homes or to other schools.
1944	20	
1945		Not recorded but would have been about 20 in view of the school closing in July 1946.
1946	8	Recorded for May. The school closed in July.

Appendix 6

Reference Sources for Information on Some Major WW2 Incidents in and Around Mannings Heath

Incident	**September 1939. High explosive bomb at Prongers Corner on the road to Monks Common.**
References	Aircraft Crashes and Bombing in the Cowfold Area During WW2. - at: cowfoldhistorysociety.org.uk
Incident	**September 1940. JU88 bomber shot down over Great Ventors Farm, Monks Common.**
References	Memories of Mannings Heath. By Tony Turner, ISBN 980-0-9540857-2-8.
	Sussex History Forum. - at: sussexhistoryforum.co.uk/index
Incident	**September 1940. The devastating bombing of Colgate with the loss of five lives.**
References	Colgate Roll of Honour. - at: roll-of-honour.com/Sussex/Colgate.htm.
Incident	**The occupation of Newells, Monks Common, by large number of Canadian troops and a number of other military units.**
References	Canadian Military Headquarters (CMQ) Reports (145 reports). - at: cmp-cpm.forces.gc.ca
	Canadian Scottish 'Pipes for Freedom'. - at: pipesforfreedom.com/webtxt/0513
	Vancouver Island University – The Canadian Letters and Images Project. - at: canadianletters.ca/content/document-15788

April 2007. Newsletter "Pioneering" A.M.PC To PC. - at: royalpioneerscorps.co.uk/newsletters

North Shore Regiment History. Royal New Brunswick Regiment (North Shore) – at: gnb.ca/0007/Heritage/Regiment/chp5i.htm

Soldier, POW, Partisan. My experiences during the battle of France, June-September 1944. Canadian Military History, Volume 9, Number 2 pp91-104. By Don Learmont, North Nova Scotia Highlanders.

103rd Heavy AA Regiment Overlord Training. - at: wikivisually.com/103rd_Heavy_Anti-Aircraft_Regiment_Royal_Artillery#Training_Training_for_Overlord

Incident	**March 1943. The RAF bomber crash and the destruction of High Beeches, Handcross.**
References	Slaugham, Handcross, Pease Pottage, Warninglid & Staplefield Archives. -at: slaughamarchives.org
	The Halifax and High Beeches. Ashdown Forest Living article by Clive Smith. December 2018. -at: ashdownforestliving.co.uk
Incident	**February 1945. RAF bomber crash on Mannings Heath golf course.**
References	The Cliff White Collection – Horsham. The War Years. Volume 6: Village Life. West Sussex Record Office AM585/7.
	Aviation Safety Network. - at: aviation-safety.net/wikibase/wiki.php?id=164976
	Royal Air Force Commands Archive. - at: rafcommands.co/archive/05603.php

References

The references used are of two types: -

- Those having a specific reference number, as listed in the text where the reference is used.

- Those held by the West Sussex Record Office that have been used to inform the text but which may not be identified specifically within the text.

Both types are listed within this "Reference" document.

References

No.	Title	Notes
1	Mannings Heath C. of E. School: Head Teacher Log Book from Sept. 10th, 1883 to July 26th, 1946.	Held by West Sussex Record Office as reference E/143B/12/3. Three volumes of Log Book and one volume of the Register of Admissions, Progress and Withdrawals for 858 pupils. (See Ref. 52 for the Register)
2	A Digest of Parochial Returns Made to the Select Committee of the House of Commons Appointed to Inquire into the Education of the Poor.	House of Commons Session 1818. Ordered to be printed 1 April 1819 and to be preserved in the Bodleian Library, Oxford. Available as a digitised Google eBook.
3	Education Enquiry. Abstract of the Answers and Returns made Pursuant to An Address of the House of Commons dated 24th May, 1833. England and Wales.	Ordered by the House of Commons to be printed 20 March 1835. An original copy available from University of Michigan, USA. Available as a digitised Google eBook.
4	1841 England, Wales and Scotland Census.	Data extracted from the Findmypast database held at findmypast.co.uk.
5	Rural Rides In The Counties. (15 English counties with economical and political observations.)	By William Cobbett. Re-issued by Cambridge University Press in 2009. ISBN 978-1-108-00408-4.
6	Emptages of Thanet (Five centuries of family history).	Published by Susan Morris et al., at emptageofthanet.co.uk.
7	The Peel Web – a Web of English History. 1760 to 1830.	Intellectual property owner and publisher – Dr Marjie Bloy at www.historyhome.co.uk.
8	Riots and Civil Disorder in England – 1830 Riots.	www.en.wikipedia.org.
9	The Peel Web – Rural Unrest in the 1830s.	See Ref. 7 for source details.
10	Swing Riots in Sussex – Agrarian Disturbances in the Winter of 1830.	By Nigel Bowles as his BA thesis at University of Manchester. Held by the West Sussex Record Office as MP1845.

References

No.	Title	Notes
11	Captain Swing Riots, 1830.	By R.L. Burgess. West Sussex History No. 63, April 1999. Held by the West Sussex Record Office as Lib. 16404/63.
12	Swing Riots – Power, Politics and Protest. The growth of political rights in Britain the 19th Century.	Hosted by the National Archives at nationalalchives.gov.uk/education/politics and accessed through learningcurve.gov.uk/politics/.
13	The Causes of the Swing Riots.	By Jonathan Nason as his BSc thesis at University of Birmingham. Held by the West Sussex Record Office as MP 999.
14	Brighton Gazette for November and December, 1830 and January, 1831.	News Cuttings concerning Swing Riots. Brighton Gazette. Held by the West Sussex Record Office as MP 1826.
15	Finding Captain Swing: Protest, Parish Relations and the State of the Public Mind in 1830.	Published in the International Review of Social History, Volume 54, Issue 03, December 2009, pp 429-458. By Peter Jones, Dept. of History, Oxford Brookes University.
16	Machine Breakers News	Volume 1, No. 4. August 1995. Edited by Jill Chambers of Letchworth, Hertfordshire. Held by the West Sussex Record Office as Lib. 17470.
17	British Convict Transportation Registers.	1787 – 1867 database compiled by the State Library of Queensland from British Home Office records.
18	"As lated tongues bespoke": Popular Protest in South-East England, 1790-1840.	By Carl Griffin, School of Geographical Sciences at the University of Bristol. Published in November, 2001.
19	History of the House of Commons 1820-1832.	Edited by D.R. Fisher, 2009. Available from Cambridge University Press and on-line at historyofparliamentonline.org.
20	Horsham's History, Volume 2.	By Jeremy Knight, Curator, Horsham Museum. Published by Horsham Museum, Nov. 2016. ISBN-10:1902484304, ISBN-13:978-1902484303.
21	Ships Eliza, Proteus and others.	Data provided by Geoffrey Sharman and available through rootsweb.ancestry.com.

No.	Title	Notes
22	Executed Today.	Blog hosted at executedtoday.com.
23	Capital Punishment UK.	Authored by Richard Clark and published as a web site at capitalpunishmentuk.org.
24	Socialism, radicalism and nostalgia. Social Criticism in Britain 1775-1830.	William Stafford. Published by Cambridge University Press, 1987. ISBN 0 521 32792.
25	London Road Methodist Church, Horsham 1832-2007.	Written and researched by Sue Checkland and other Church members. Published in 2008 by the London Road Methodist Church. Copies held in the Horsham Museum and The British Library, St Pancras.
26	The role of soldiers in the origins of Wesleyan Methodism in Brighton and other towns on the Sussex Coast.	By Michael R. Hickman and published in Sussex Archaeological Collections 143 (2005) pp 257-66.
27	A History of the County of Sussex, Volume 6 Part 3.	For the Bramber Rape (North Eastern Part) including Crawley New Town. Edited by T.P. Hudson. Published in 1987 and available online as British History Online at british-history.ac.uk.
28	Brighton Circuit Methodist Records.	Held by the East Sussex Record Office as reference NMA5/1/1/1 – General Circuit Book.
29	Register of Births and Baptisms.	At the Horsham Independent Chapel in the Parish of Horsham, Sussex from 1784 to 1800. Data held by BMDregsters.co.uk in association with the National Archives. TNA reference RG4/Piece 4419/Folio 11.
30	Memories of Mannings Heath – memories of past times in the West Sussex village of Mannings Heath.	By Tony Turner and first published in November, 2010. ISBN 980-0-9540857-2-8.

References

No.	Title	Notes
31	Elementary Education Parish Files – Nuthurst.	National Archives reference ED 2/442 being a subset of records ED2 – Education Department and Successors: Elementary Education Parish Files – Nuthurst.
32	The Long Revolution.	By Raymond Williams published in 1961 by Chatto and Windus. ISBN: 0-14-020762-7.
33	The History of Education in England in the Nineteenth Century.	Available on the Know Britain web site at: know-britain.com/general/education_in_england 2.html.
34	A Historical Perspective on Methodist Involvement in School Education after Wesley.	By G.M. Best and hosted on the web site: methodist.org.uk/education.
35	Sunday School.	Hosted at: en.wikipedia.org/wiki/Sunday_school.
36	Victorian Childhood – Themes and Variations.	By Thomas E. Jordan. Published by State University of New York Press in 1987. ISBN 0-88706-544-9. Available via Google eBooks.
37	Plan of the Wesleyan Methodist Preachers in the Dorking and Horsham Circuit.	1847-8, 1857 and 1856-57 plans held in the Horsham Methodist Church records and provided by Sue Checkland.
38	Education in England: a brief history (Chapter 2).	"Towards a state system of education". By Derek Gillard MA Dip. Ed. Retired middle school headmaster. First published June 1998. Most recent update 2011. Available at eductionengland.org.uk.
39	Education in England: a brief history (Timeline)	By Derek Gillard MA Dip. Ed. See ref. 38.
40	Education in England: a brief history (Chapter 3).	"1860-1890 Class divisions". By Derek Gillard MA Dip.Ed.
41	Albery's Monthly Illustrated Journal for September, 1869.	"Opening of the New Wesleyan Chapel at Mannings Heath, Nuthurst". Held by Horsham Museum.

No.	Title	Notes
42	Home Office Ecclesiastical Census Returns 1851.	For Horsham, including Mannings Heath and Nuthurst. Held by the National Archives as ref. HO 129/87.
43	"...trying to serve both God and Mamon?"	West Sussex County Times article by H. Browning. 8th June, 1973.
44	Minute Book of the Trustees of Mannings Heath Methodist Church. (1951-1972).	Dorking and Horsham Methodist Circuit and Constituent Churches: Records. Held by Surrey History Centre, Woking. Ref.2657/7/2. This is a closed record so only a summary is available.
45	Photohistory-sussex.	Photohistory-sussex.co.uk/HorshamPhotgrsBG.htm including an extract from Kellys Directory.
46	Probate Calendar for England and Wales 1858-1959.	Hosted by findmypast.co.uk. Downloaded 17.01 2017.
47	National Archives. Nuthurst Parish Files.	Education Department and Successor: Elementary Education, Parish Files. Sussex West. Elementary education parish files. Nuthurst. Ref. ED2/442.
48	Horsham and Dorking Circuit Schedule Book.	Held in the Surrey History Centre, Woking. Ref. 2657/2/2.
49	Horsham and Mannings Heath Methodist Records.	Minute Book of the trustees of Mannings Heath Chapel and School. Ref. 456/10/1. Minute 12/7/1895. Held in the Surrey History Centre, Woking.
50	Horsham and Dorking Circuit Records.	Circuit County Trusts Minute Book. Mannings Heath 1909-1929. Ref 456/8/2. Held in the Surrey History Centre, Woking.
51	Scholars and Slates – Sussex Schools in the 1880s.	By Steve Johnson and Kim Leslie. Prepared on behalf of the West Sussex County Council, as part of the 100 year celebrations, with sponsorship from Barclays Bank and under the direction of Richard Bunker, Director of Education. ISBN 086260 167 3.

References

No.	Title	Notes
52	Mannings Heath School Register.	Register of Admissions, Progress and Withdrawals, 1883-1946. Held by the West Sussex Record Office as part of the school log books reference E143B/12/1.2 and 3.
53	Southwater Victorians – Lives and Portraits.	Compiled and published by the Southwater Local History Group in October 2013. Copies available from southwaterhistory.co.uk.
54	Kathleen Langley Notes.	Unpublished notes prepared by the Mannings Heath historian Kathleen Langley and provided to the author in 2012.
55	The Nutters – a history.	A history of Nuthurst Cricket Club from 1830 to 2004. By David Boorman. See pitchero.com/clubs/nuthurstcricketclub.
56	Diary of Mrs Augusta Bigg 1872-1875.	Transcript held in the West Sussex Record Office as AM913/2/7.
57	The Story of Swallowfield – a short history of the Bigg family in West Sussex and Australia.	Written and published by A.R. Turner with a first edition in April, 2001. ISBN 0-9540857-0-1. Copies may be obtained from the author at 11, Lime Kiln Road Mannings Heath, RH13 6JH.
58	Diary of Miss Augusta Bigg 1880-1884.	Transcript held in the West Sussex Record Office as AM913/2/10.
59	Exeter & Plymouth Gazette 12th February, 1884.	Report of the Honiton Board of Guardians recording the appointment of Louisa Buck as schoolmistress in the House.
60	Memories of the 1860s by Frederick Fuller.	Lent to the author by Mark Scrase Dickins of Coolhurst Manor. Copied to him by Mario Fuller (mario.fuller@virgin.net), a descendent of Frederick Fuller.
61	Conveyance of the land for Mannings Heath School.	By Charles Scrace Dickins of Coolhurst and dated 11th June, 1883. Held by West Sussex Record Office as reference Par. 143/25/1.

No.	Title	Notes
62	Primary Object Lessons. A Manual of Elementary Instruction.	By N.A. Calkins. The fifteenth edition published by Harper Brothers, New York in 1870. As an aid to "Training the senses and developing the faculties of children."
63	Plan of Mannings Heath School.	Data extracted from the property valuation report (circa 1900). Report reference 8574. Held by the National Archives in ED21/17544.
64	Government Circular to HM Inspectors of Schools.	Issued on 16th January, 1878. Held in West Sussex Record Office as Par 203/25/14.
65	Ruri-Decanal Parish Magazine.	For Storrington (Div 11), Diocese of Chichester for a number of Parishes, including Nuthurst. 1885–1890. Extracts relating to Mannings Heath School made available to the author by David Hilliam of the Nuthurst Local History Society.
66	Nuthurst, Mannings Heath Church of England School.	Board of Education, Local Education Authority and School Manager's correspondence and reports from 1893 to 1931. National Archives References: ED 21/41261, ED 21/62344 and ED 21/17544.
67	School Attendance 1880-1939.	A study of policy and practice in response to the problem of truancy. By Nicola Sheldon, Harris Manchester College. PhD submission, Trinity Term, 2007.
68	London Metropolitan Archives Information Leaflet Number 32.	"The evacuation of children from the County of London during the Second World War." Published November 1997 and updated 2010.
69	Government Evacuation Schemes and their Effect on Schoolchildren in Sheffield in the Second World War.	By Audrey Ann Elcock as a PhD thesis. University of Sheffield, April 1999.
70	West Sussex County Times.	1st September, 1939. "Horsham Waiting To Welcome Evacuees."
71	CEES – Bringing Learning to Life.	Cambridgeshire Environmental Education Service at www.cees.org.uk/memories_letters.htm.

References

No.	Title	Notes
72	Evacuee Admissions Register.	For Mannings Heath School. Held by West Sussex Record Office as E/143A/13/1/2.
73	St Andrew's School, Nuthurst Log Book.	Head Teacher's Log Book for Nuthurst School. January 1923 to February 1947. Held by the West Sussex Record Office as Reference E/143A/12/4.
74	The Pillbox Study Group.	www.pillbox-study-group.org.
75	The Cliff White Collection – Horsham: The War Years.	Volume 6: Village Life. Held by the West Sussex Record Office as Reference AM 585/7.
76	The Story of the Home Front in West Sussex 1939-1945.	By Alan Readman, Lead Manager, Archives, West Sussex Record Office, February 2012. Available at www.westsussexpast.org.uk.

Mannings Heath School History. Data Sources

WSRO – West Sussex Records Office, Chichester

Reference/ Identification	Title
Par/143/1/5/3	Register of Burials 1875-1958
Par/143/3/1	Incumbent: Registers of Preachers and Services – Mannings Heath, Church of the Good Shepherd: Service Register.
Par/143/7/2	Inventory of the Church of the Good Shepherd (Jan. 1930).
Par/143/7/8	Incumbent: Miscellaneous – Photographs of book given to Miss Augusta Bigg.
Par/143/12/1	Vestry Minutes 1895-1922.
Par/143/14/1	Parochial Church Council: Minutes (vol 1) (1941-1958).
Par/143/14/2	Parochial Church Council: Minutes (vol 2) (1920-1939).
Par/143/25/4	Minute Book of the Managers of the Nuthurst & Mannings Heath Schools 1903-1936.
Par/143/25/1	Conveyance, with copy, of the Mannings Heath School site.
Par/143/25/2	Deed of declaration of authenticity of 25/1 by the Incumbent. 1906.
Par/143/25/3	Conveyance of land for the Mannings Heath school house. 1886.
Par/143/49/1	Parish Council Minute Book. (vol 1) (1894-1953).
Par/14/38/2	Electors List for the district of Mannings Heath. 1925.
Add Mss 18811	Will of Robert Reading. 1911.
E/143B/6/1	Letter from Director of Education. Tarring playground. 1937.
E/143B/6/2	Letter about school fence. 1937.
E/143B/17/2	Letter about art instruction. 1936.
E/143B/17/3	Letters of complaint about the Head. 1935.
E/143B/17	Headmaster letters.
E/143B/19/1	Notes on teaching. 1921.
E/143B/19/2	Copies of HMI reports. 1931 & 1937.
E143A/1/1	Managers Minute Book (1936-1967) (See Par/143/25/4 above).
E/143B19/3	Photos of Mannings Heath School.

References

Reference/Identification	Title
AM 585/7	The Cliff White Collection, Horsham: The War Years vol 6 Village Life.
MP 8342	West Sussex Gazette articles on villages in West Sussex, Mannings Heath published 13th December, 1979.
RD/HO/16/1	Plan No. 2431 House on Goldings Hill.
RD/HO/16/1	Plan No. 2557 Temporary Bungalow, Goldings Road.
SP 712	Sale Particulars – Old Chapel.
MSS 14823	West Sussex County Council Scheme for establishment of an Education Committee. 07 Feb. '03.
E/102/1/7	Extracts from Managers Minutes 1919-1920.
E/102/1/8	Extracts from Managers Minutes 1921-1922.
E/102/1/9	Extracts from Mangers Minutes 1922-1925.
Lib 17996	West Sussex Education Committee handbook for 1932-1933.
WOC/CC2/32	Council Proceedings & Public Documents issued by the County Council. Indexed agenda papers, 1920/21.
WOC/CC2/33	As above, 1921/22.
WOC/CC2/34	As above, 1922/23.
WOC/CC2/35	As above, 1923/24.
WOC/CC2/36	As above, 1924/25.
WOC/CC2/59	As above, 1943/44.
WOC/CC2/60	As above, 1944/45.
Hurst Mss Acc 4539/122	School at Nuthurst (1860).
E/143A/12/1	Nuthurst School Log Book 1863-1885.
E/143A/12/4	Nuthurst School Log Book Jan 1923-Feb 1947.
PH 26118/135, 6,7	Wanderings in Sussex. Vol. 5, Western Division. "A collection of photographs of old houses." By John H.B. Fletcher.
Add Mss 18811	Will of Robert Reading 26/08/1911.

CPSIA information can be obtained
at www.ICGtesting.com
Printed in the USA
LVHW060119010522
717630LV00011B/645